"In *Shifting Shadows*, you wil
of God at work that will enco
—L

of *The Yes Effect*

"A beautiful, raw testimony of the radical grace of Christ in Herman's life and how God continues to save others through Pastor Mendoza and his ministry. I am blessed to know him!"

—Kevin Palau, president and CEO
of the Luis Palau Association

"To spend five minutes with Herman Mendoza now, it would be challenging to imagine him spending five years in federal prison for dealing illicit drugs. Since our paths crossed, I have witnessed his efforts in reaching young people for Christ and his commitment to impact our society with his testimony. In *Shifting Shadows*, we can grasp the essence of God's unwavering grace."

—Allan Houston, former two-time NBA All-Star
and assistant general manager of the New York Knicks

"Herman Mendoza's testimony is an amazing story of how the grace and love of Jesus transformed his life, bringing him from a life of crime and prison into gospel ministry, healing his marriage, and making his family whole."

—Dr. George O. Wood, chairman
of the World Assemblies of God Fellowship

"Usually people don't admit to their frailties, failures, and lives of wickedness, but in *Shifting Shadows*, Herman Mendoza tells it all. From a busted drug dealer to a prominent and faithful servant of God, he bares his soul. It is a poignant and captivating story with redeeming value for a worldwide audience."

—Raymond Joseph, author and former ambassador of Haiti
to the United States

"Herman's story is a powerful example of the way God restores the years that the locusts have eaten. Through Christ and the power of the gospel, we see love, redemption, and freedom born out of greed, emptiness, and bondage. In a culture riddled with addictions, this is an uplifting story worthy of our attention."

—Candy Marballi, president and CEO of the Prayer Covenant

"This raw, utterly engaging narrative of Pastor Mendoza's journey demonstrates how God takes the torn pieces of life and creates a beautiful tapestry of His love and mercy to reveal His glory!"

—Nick Brino, local sales manager of Salem Media Group, DC

"Caution: If you start reading this book at 10 P.M., you might not get much sleep that night. I had set aside only a short period to read this book, but I became so engrossed in the ups and downs of Herman's life story that I ended up pushing my schedule back. This memoir crosses all cultures and shows how God's grace can rescue a lost soul regardless of how hard he or she hits rock bottom."

—Joel Freeman, PhD, director and producer of *Return to Glory*;
former NBA chaplain

"It is so exciting to read this testimony of the extremity and the availability of God's grace. Jesus is not only in the cathedral, He is in the classroom, the hospital room, the courtroom, and the prison cell. Pastor Mendoza is a trophy of God's grace, and I am blessed to be a witness of his transformed life. I hope this book will convince you that hope is just a prayer away!"

—Reverend Pete Richardson, lead pastor of Grace Ministries,
Promise Church

"*Shifting Shadows* exemplifies the work of grace in a life that has tasted both the giddy heights of sin and the lowest depths of desperation. Once I began to read, I was hooked and could not put it down. Herman Mendoza's account is riveting from start to finish."

—Reverend Lloyd Pulley, senior pastor of Calvary Chapel,
Old Bridge, New Jersey

"I highly recommend *Shifting Shadows*. Herman Mendoza has a thrilling story that speaks boldly to the urban issues of today."

—Dimas Salaberrios, author of *Street God*

"This book is amazing and heartfelt from beginning to end. My utmost respect for Herman Mendoza. To be able to put his past behind him and give back to those who need it is truly an act of a hero."

—Miguelina Puello, retired NYPD sergeant and adjunct professor

SHIFTING
SHADOWS

SHIFTING SHADOWS

*How a New York Drug Lord Found Freedom
in the Last Place He Expected*

Herman Mendoza

BETHANYHOUSE

a division of Baker Publishing Group
Minneapolis, Minnesota

© 2020 by Herman A. Mendoza

Published by Bethany House Publishers
11400 Hampshire Avenue South
Bloomington, Minnesota 55438
www.bethanyhouse.com

Bethany House Publishers is a division of
Baker Publishing Group, Grand Rapids, Michigan

Printed in the United States of America

ISBN 978-0-7642-3616-7
ISBN 978-0-7642-3617-4 (Spanish edition)

Library of Congress Cataloging-in-Publication Control Number: 2019055367

Unless otherwise indicated, Scripture quotations are from THE HOLY BIBLE, NEW INTERNATIONAL VERSION®, NIV® Copyright © 1973, 1978, 1984, 2011 by Biblica, Inc.® Used by permission. All rights reserved worldwide.

Scripture quotations identified ESV are from The Holy Bible, English Standard Version® (ESV®), copyright © 2001 by Crossway, a publishing ministry of Good News Publishers. Used by permission. All rights reserved. ESV Text Edition: 2016

Scripture quotations identified KJV are from the King James Version of the Bible.

Scripture quotations identified NKJV are from the New King James Version®. Copyright © 1982 by Thomas Nelson. Used by permission. All rights reserved.

Scripture quotations identified TLB are from The Living Bible, copyright © 1971. Used by permission of Tyndale House Publishers, Inc., Carol Stream, Illinois 60188. All rights reserved.

This book recounts events in the life of Herman Mendoza according to the author's recollection and information from the author's perspective. While all the stories are true, some names, dialogue, and identifying details have been changed to protect the privacy of those involved.

Cover design by Dan Pitts
Cover photo by Edwin Rodriguez/Kiss Digital
Photo on page 242 by Ramysh Bangali

Author represented by WordServe Literary

20 21 22 23 24 25 26   7 6 5 4 3 2 1

I dedicate this book to my Lord and Savior, Jesus Christ.
This book was written to bring glory to you, my Lord,
and as a testimony of your transforming power.

In memory of my loving parents,
Fernando and Maria Mendoza.

Contents

Every good and perfect gift
is from above,
coming down from the Father
of the heavenly lights,
who does not change
like shifting shadows.

JAMES 1:17

FOREWORD

Wherever you are on your journey, reading this book is a side trip worth taking. Maybe you picked this up in desperation—you're hanging on by a thread, trying to save your very life. Or maybe you're just appeasing someone who seems to actually care about you and thinks Herman's story might help make sense of your mess. Whatever the condition of your heart and life as you begin this book, I encourage you to read it to the end. It's part cautionary tale and part testament to hope and grace—I couldn't turn the pages fast enough!

No matter the twists and tangles in your life's tapestry, don't give up. Like my friend Herman, you might be looking at the wrong side. Someday you may discover that on the other side of the fabric God has been creating a beautiful picture all along—no pain wasted, no teardrop unseen. It may all come together beautifully when you realize those knots and snarls were integral to the profound richness of your purpose. You might one day say, "Oh, *that's* why!"

I know from my own suffering that this may make no sense to you *now*. You might be thinking, *How could any good come of my messed-up life? How can this possibly turn around? Scars this deep can't heal, much less become something of beauty, purpose, or even healing to others . . . can they?*

On the other hand, you might have your act totally together. Things are going great. If so, I'm happy for you. But read this book to arm yourself for the possibility of everything changing in a whirlwind of devastation. Prepare your heart for the climb back up out of the abyss. Herman's odyssey can inspire you to have renewed hope and restored faith that *anything* can be redeemed.

Perhaps you have a friend or loved one who is in the midst of deep despair, caught in a downward spiral that can only end in destruction. Sharing Herman's book might encourage them: "Here, read this—it's by a guy who sank so low, just taking the next breath was a victory." As is often said, where there's life, there's still hope. You'll believe it after reading this dramatic account of Herman's life.

This is a true, powerful, and engaging narrative with a potentially life-changing message. There is a reason you are now holding it in your hands. I know, love, and respect Herman Mendoza. Or at least I thought I knew him before reading his whole gritty saga. Now I know it to be even more true that he is the real deal—a man of strong faith with a sincere heart to honor God and help others. For years now he has traveled tirelessly across the world championing the cause of children. Children! Who would have thought such a transformation was even possible? Frank Warren is said to have written, "It's the children the world almost breaks who grow up to save it." Herman was just such a child. But he is now a full-fledged warrior for the weak and vulnerable, the poorest of the poor who suffer the most but cannot speak up for themselves. How did that happen? You owe it to yourself to read Herman's remarkable story of unlikely grace. Your eyes may well be opened to the shadows of grace in your own life story.

What a wonderful God we have—he is the Father of our Lord Jesus Christ, the source of every mercy, and the one who so wonderfully comforts and strengthens us in our hardships and trials. And why does he do this? So that when others are troubled, needing our sympathy and encouragement, we can pass on to them this same help and comfort God has given us.

2 Corinthians 1:3–4 TLB

—Dr. Wess Stafford, president emeritus,
Compassion International

A NOTE FROM HERMAN

The story you are about to read is my testimony. My intentions are not to glamorize sin or justify the poor decisions I made in my past—I take full responsibility for my actions. Instead, I simply want to share about the hope and transforming power that can be found through Jesus Christ. I've tried to write about events, locations, and conversations to the best of my memory. Some of the names and locations have been changed to protect individuals' privacy. My hope is that this book will help you navigate through your life journey and into a relationship with the one who saved my soul: Jesus.

PROLOGUE

Mr. Goldstein was everything I hated. Tall and skinny, he had "Grade A nerd" written all over him. His New Jersey accent and his gravelly voice grated on my nerves. But the thing I hated the most about him was that he was the kind of teacher who thought he had everyone pegged.

Mr. Goldstein looked at me like I was a nobody—like I wouldn't amount to anything. But he was wrong. Sure, I was in fifth grade and hadn't hit my growth spurt yet, but I had my own crew. Kids listened to me. I was a somebody, and someday soon I was gonna make him realize it.

When he left the classroom, I took the opportunity to dazzle the other kids with my spot-on impression of the human orangutan. I made my voice real deep, and I let my arms dangle as if the appendages were too long for me to control.

"Listen here, class." I clapped my hands as if to get their attention. "Back when I was a kid, we had to eat dung just like the Aztecs, just to survive the winter."

I didn't hear the door open or Mr. Goldstein stride over to me with his stealthy ninja steps. When I noticed the other kids looking up at him, it was too late. My archnemesis squared his narrow shoulders and reached out an impossibly long arm to grab me.

"What did you just say?"

His raspy voice sounded choked . . . like maybe he was going to cry. I wanted to think it was because I'd knocked him down a notch or two in front of the class, but his voice often sounded like that; it was another one of the things that irritated me about him. I tilted my chin up and laughed in his face.

"You didn't hear me the first time? You want me to do it again?"

A few of the other kids snickered.

He shook me before shoving me back down in my chair.

Forget you! I wanted to scream. I'd had enough of him too. I took a swing at his jaw. I may have been only ten, but I was arguably the most influential student in P.S. 019, our school. He had no idea who he was dealing with.

Mr. Goldstein's face reddened and his eyes narrowed. He swatted at me, but I slapped his hand away. It irked me that I had to kowtow to him just because he wore a stupid, ugly tie and had a degree. Who was he to tell me what to do?

I took another swing. He stopped it with one hand, then grabbed my neck with the other and slammed my face against the desk. My nose started pouring out blood. Injured but not broken.

Holding me there, with my face smashed against graffitied wood, he growled, "The way you're going, Herman, you're not going to amount to anything. You'll wind up in gangs, or jail, and you will die!"

1

THE CORONA BOYS

"What do I gotta do?" I asked, swinging my pocketknife between my thumb and forefinger.

I was in the running to join the Corona Boys, and I wanted in bad. The first gang I'd started, Devils Inc., disbanded before I'd even made it to sixth grade. Now that I was in junior high, I wanted to join an established gang. There were loads in the area, but two really stood out from the rest: the Corona Boys and the Lefrak City Crew. Joining either gang would have been okay, but the Corona Boys were in my territory in Queens, New York, and I was the loyal type.

"You can cool it, Herm. We know who you are. You're down for anything, right?"

I nodded. Just once. No need to look too eager.

"All right. You're in."

One of the boys tossed me a black-and-white bandana. I couldn't believe it. It was way easier than I'd expected.

I was a Corona Boy.

That meant, no matter what happened, we had each other's backs.

"A. R.!" One of the guys called me as he tore across the school-yard.

A. R., short for "A-Rocker," was my street name because of my break-dancing skills. I could hear scuffling ahead of us, but the visual evidence of the fight was blocked from view by a line of spectators. I sprinted after him.

Pushing through the screaming throng, I stumbled into the open area by the basketball courts. The Lefrak City Crew was laying into one of our guys. I jumped into the fray, fists flying.

I swung at one of the smaller guys in the enemy gang. My first target was still older and taller than me but looked like he had no idea what to do with his hands.

I felt my knuckles connect with the soft flesh of his cheek before hitting bone. *That should throw him off balance.* I went for the gut. If I winded

Me in my early teenage years

him, I could take him down. Kids were cheering. My body was pumping adrenaline. It was great!

"Ooph!"

My fist sank into his abdomen; he didn't have time to steel himself against the blow. The air left his lungs in a powerful blast, and he crumpled.

I wanted to take a second to rejoice in my victory, but two guys dragged me from behind and threw me on the ground. My nerves ignited as the skin on my shoulders scraped pavement. I scrambled to my feet and jogged backward away from them, fists at the ready.

A quick sweep of the schoolyard told me this wasn't going to be some quick, thirty-second throw down with a clear winner. This was mayhem. An all-out gang war. Kids screamed and chanted names from both sides.

The school's security guards swept past the mass of shouting students. Their whistles blared as they tried to come between a few of us, but we were not backing down. Teachers and students started screaming, "Call the police!"

But it still didn't stop us.

Blood ran down my face. I tried to make a fist, but my knuckles were bruised and swollen. My lungs felt like they were on fire every time I breathed, but I wouldn't give up.

And then I heard sirens. I had to get out of there if I didn't want to get nabbed.

I took off, scrambling to lose myself in the crowd of students that had stayed to watch.

As soon as the cops arrived everything halted. They hauled a bunch of the Lefrak City Crew and a few of our guys away.

I heard they sent them to disciplinary detention at the local precinct. I was glad I wasn't there, sitting on a hard metal bench, waiting for my parents to show up and administer a worse beating than I'd just received. Instead, I was a free man, walking down 102nd Street, a little shaken but proud of my escape.

2

A BITE OF THE APPLE

Marijuana was a forbidden fruit, which, of course, made it all the more tempting. All the guys I knew who smoked pot seemed pretty cool, possibly because they were all older than me. But I liked to believe it was the pot, because if I got my hands on some, I could be just like them.

Everybody said it was bad for you, but I still wanted to try it. Just once, so I could decide for myself.

When some of the older guys in the neighborhood asked me to join them in the alley one night, I knew exactly what it was about. One of them—Elvis, or Cid, or Ruben probably—had gotten hold of a joint. I figured whether I ended up liking it or not, it didn't matter. If I smoked a joint with them, I'd be one of them—rolling with the big kids.

Elvis was in eleventh grade, and he lived on the edge. He was always daring us to do something wild and crazy, but never something he wasn't willing to do himself.

Ruben was the oldest in the group and tall, really tall, with black hair and a dark complexion. He was the toughest guy I'd ever met. Lucky for me he was a friend and not an enemy.

Cid was the nickname we'd given Cedric. He was wild, always cracking jokes. There was no guessing what would come out of his mouth, or what crazy idea he'd follow through on.

I followed the guys into the alley that separated 102nd and 101st Street—a stone's throw from my house. Cid pulled a skinny joint from his pocket and lit it, taking a long, slow drag. The end of the joint burned red in the darkness.

My adrenaline had kicked in well before we had turned the corner into the alley. The crunch of gravel underfoot grew quieter with each step as my pulse thundered louder and louder in my ears. The alley was unlit, and the night sky boasted only a sliver of a moon. We were sheltered by the blackness. On the other side of the houses, streetlights illuminated Corona's nightlife. No one knew that just fifty feet from the street, Cid had just handed me my first joint. I held it between quivering lips and took my first puff.

I inhaled and instantly felt like I was choking. It was disgusting. I didn't cough, though. Instead, I held the smoke in my lungs until I felt they would burst. I exhaled slowly through pursed lips, the way I had seen Cid do it. I was surprised that I didn't feel an immediate high. I took another couple of puffs; I didn't want to look like a chump. And before I knew it, I was laughing. Minutes later, we all were. Cid had always been funny, but tonight everything he said and did was hilarious. Elvis and Ruben too. Those guys could be stand-up comics.

"Man, I'm hungry," Elvis said. "We should grab some pizza or something."

I suddenly realized I was starving. "Cool. But I don't got much money. Let's just hit up the store on the corner. Grab some potato chips."

We crept out of the dark alleyway and ran down the street, shoving each other into parked cars, playing chicken in the traffic. Everything about that night seemed like an adventure. I was no longer just some kid in seventh grade. I was hanging with guys who were practically adults.

I stayed out later than normal; I didn't want my mami to smell the weed on my clothes. We smoked some regular cigarettes and walked the streets of Corona. When I finally crept up to my house, our dog, Mosquito, a great Dane, started sniffing. I scratched behind his ears and tried to act normal in case anyone was watching.

Mami was still up when I walked in, sitting in the kitchen getting something ready for the next day. She rubbed her tired eyes as I passed by on the way to my room, but she looked up for just a moment and I thought I caught a glimmer of suspicion, but she said nothing.

Poor Mami was perpetually tired when she was home—a result of long hours at the lamp factory. She had to leave early in the morning to get there, so even if she had concerns, it wasn't worth an argument or a lecture at this time of night. If she did suspect anything, she would probably wait until Papi was home on the weekend and have him talk to me.

I liked talking with Papi, even if it meant listening to a lecture. He would usually only talk to me while we worked together on his car. He'd tell me about how it all fit together, and then slowly he'd ask questions and get me talking. It was too bad we didn't get to see him much; he worked in New Jersey, about an hour's drive away, which meant he was only home a couple of days a week. It was the sacrifice he made to provide for his sons, Gabriel, Emilio, Fabian, Dante, and me.

It only took a couple of weeks for me to feel like a veteran pot smoker. Elvis, Ruben, Cid, and I met daily to share a joint in the back alley after school. I wasn't even worried about Mami or Papi finding out anymore. *What are they gonna do about it? Yell at me? Paddle my backside? I can take it.*

"Yo, Herman!" Jayson waved from the alleyway with Cid and Ruben behind him. I'd known Jayson for a few years. He lived a block over from my house. Like most of us in the area, Jayson was Dominican—he was lighter skinned like me and had the same taste in clothes: jeans, sneakers, and tank tops. He was a crazy kid with a wicked temper, but I liked him.

I jogged over to the guys, curious what Jayson was doing with them. He met me on the sidewalk, throwing an arm over my shoulders and dragging me along behind the row houses. "Ruben tells me you got a joint and you'll share."

I nodded, the back of my head knocking against the solid muscle of his forearm. Jayson was a Goliath, easily six feet tall and ready to pick a fight with anybody over anything. He'd usually win too.

I pulled out the joint I'd bought earlier that day. Jayson plucked it from my fingers and flicked open his lighter.

"Don't mind if I do." He grinned.

We passed around the joint, laughing at some of the stupid things we'd done that day.

"You ever tried coke?" Jayson asked out of the blue.

Cid and I shook our heads, but Ruben shrugged as if to imply he'd tried it, and it was no big deal.

"I know where we can get some . . . if you want to try some with me."

I was curious. I'd heard a lot about it over the last few weeks. If it was as good as they said, I wanted to give it a go. "I'd try it with you."

Jayson slapped me five. "Deal."

It took him a few days to get his hands on a little package of coke, but once he did, true to his word, Jayson found me.

He invited me to join him in the back alley off Ninety-Second Street. He cut up a couple of lines on a piece of cardboard, rolled up a piece of paper, and took a hit before passing it to me. I copied what I had seen Jayson do. It took almost no time at all for a feeling of euphoria to overtake me.

I liked smoking pot, but this was a whole new kind of thrill. My mind was racing, but not in confusion.

I felt like I could run faster, hit harder, and jump higher than I ever had before. I'd always been a pretty popular kid. Some friends of my mami even called me a charmer. But with the white stuff coursing through me, I was convinced I could charm the stockings off a supermodel. It was a shame to waste the feeling in some dark alley. I left Jayson behind and strutted home, nodding and smiling at everyone I passed.

Another good thing about coke was that Mami wouldn't be able to smell it on me. Yep, cocaine was the way to go.

Within days my focus shifted. I was getting tired of the Corona Boys; we didn't share the same drug choice anymore. Though I was only in my early teens, their petty playground squabbles had started to feel a little G-rated. I didn't have time to fight the Lefrak City Crew just because they tread on my turf. Who cared? Jayson, Elvis, Cid, Ruben—they were my people, and they had the right kinds of connections.

I was getting ready to go out on Saturday morning when Mami stopped me. She seemed to suspect something was up. "Herman, you've barely been home all week. What are you doing out there? If you aren't home by eight tonight, you can forget going out at all next week."

I nodded as I sauntered down the hall to the front door. But I had no intention of heeding her words. Mami was at work all day, Monday through Friday. There was no way she could enforce a grounding.

"I'm putting Gabriel in charge!" she called after me.

I waved. "Okay, Mami. See you later."

Nuts. Gabriel would try to stop me. He had already finished high school. He needed to understand, if he tried to fill Mami's role, that I would fight him . . . or at the very least, I would refuse to listen to him. Gabriel was not the boss of me.

"Are you coming?" Jayson asked, waiting for me at the corner of 103rd Street. He held up a particularly fat little joint.

"Naw, man, not today. I'm heading to Tito's."

Jayson gave me a shrug. "Cool. Score enough for both of us?"

I nodded and took off.

Tito was a local dealer we knew who always kept his stash in his bedroom. I'd find excuses to be there so I could sneak into his room and take a little coke.

The first time I did it I was sure I'd get caught. I waited until he was high before walking down the hall, my hand on the zipper of my jeans as if to suggest that I needed to take a leak. His door squeaked as I closed it behind me before rifling through his dresser drawers. His stash wasn't even really hidden. I moved a few socks aside, and there it was. A plastic bag filled with a bunch of little cling wrap sachets.

I took a small one and stuffed it in my pocket before slowly easing that creaky door open again. As soon as I passed the door of the bathroom I resumed my normal gait. I didn't want to look like I was sneaking around. The little sachet I had stolen was only good for a couple of highs, but I would rather take my chances by repeat offending than get caught with a bigger packet.

Today, Tito passed out minutes after I got there. It was like he was begging for me to steal from him. When I got back to 103rd Street, Jayson was nowhere to be seen. His loss. I wasn't going to wait for him. I tapped out a line on the back of my hand and inhaled deeply.

Mami was waiting for me when I got home that night. I was expecting a lecture, but she looked too defeated to deliver it. I felt a twinge deep down inside. Guilt? Mami was probably the only one who could still make me feel it. I hadn't spent much time with her lately. She used to say I was the one she could rely on, her little helper.

I grabbed a glass of water and sat down beside her at the table. She rubbed her work-calloused hand over mine. "Mi niño precioso."

I smiled. I was still her precious boy.

"Te amo, Mami."

My mami was a beautiful human being. Her hair was still jet black, and her eyes still sparkled when she smiled. And despite her long hours at work every day, the house was filled with the smells of our favorite Dominican dishes.

Mami pushed a plate of fried *plátano* toward me. It was cold now but still delicious. Cocaine had the opposite effect from pot on my appetite, but I still could easily finish off whatever my mami put in front of me. No joke, her cooking could rival that of the best chef in New York.

I went to bed that night feeling more like a little boy than I had in a very long time. It was a pity it didn't last.

3

RENEGADE DEMONS

"Herm?" I felt a nudge at my side.

Abel Ramirez's voice was mellow and cool. A Latino and New Yorker, he was everything I wanted to be. He didn't take hassle from anybody, and at nineteen he was the leader of one of the coolest gangs in the area: the Renegade Demons.

Abel handed me a joint.

I took it, leaning my head against the back of the schoolyard steps and taking a long, slow drag.

Most members of the gang were a few years older than me, but for some reason they had accepted me into their crew. I, an eighth grader, had made it into one of the most hard-core gangs in the area.

It was a crisp October night. On the cold concrete steps where we sat, I slowly let out a little puff of smoke and watched it rise toward the vastness of space.

I loved these nights with the guys, chilling and talking about girls. It must have been close to midnight, but none of us were keeping track. The city had a type of music at this time of night. A rhythm produced from horns and sirens, the music of nightclubs, and the occasional rattle and screech of trains on the 7 Train subway bridge just across the yard.

Some kids claimed ghosts haunted the schoolyard at night, but I was sure the only spirits haunting this place were the Renegade Demons. No one else dared step foot on our turf.

The breeze picked up, carrying away our smoke and causing a little shower of leaves. It brought with it the sweet smell of fall. It was a perfect moment—sitting there, laughing with the boys about nothing in particular.

"Abel!" An angry shout cut across the yard.

Before anyone emerged from the shadows, we could hear him coming. His footsteps echoed on the pavement, making it unclear which direction he was coming from. Then suddenly a man stood right in front of us, baseball bat in hand.

We all scrambled to our feet, sluggish from the marijuana. Without warning, he swung his bat at Abel. I ducked. Abel ducked. We skittered backward.

I found myself crouching low by the steps, my fists at the ready. Abel started to run from the crazed intruder.

And then I heard a second shout.

Another guy came out from the shadows at the opposite side of the yard, right where Abel was heading. He pulled out a .25 pistol and took aim. Abel stopped in his tracks, then turned and started running back toward us when the shot rang out.

My heart stopped.

As Abel collapsed, it seemed as if time itself had ground to a halt. His head and arms wrenched backward, and his chest spasmed forward, pulling him toward the ground as the bullet tore a hole in his back.

My body trembled. My mind couldn't make sense of it. The cool breeze suddenly felt as cold as ice. Even the orange glow of the streetlights across the yard seemed to be swallowed up by shadows.

The man with the gun stood there, his pistol raised in front of him and his mouth a taut line. His brows pinched together. His voice was venomous as he spat out, "Next time you try messing with me, I'll kill you."

No one moved. Our fists were no match for his bullets.

Is he dead? Is he dead? Is he dead?

It seemed an eternity before Abel's attackers turned to go, but it could only have been twenty seconds or so. I had held my breath from the moment of the gunshot until the moment they turned and left.

As soon as they were out of sight, the Renegade Demons sprang into action. Our leader lay perfectly still on the frigid pavement. As we crouched around him we could see the slow rise and fall of his back and shoulders. He was still breathing.

One of the older guys, Paco, tugged Abel's shirt up, revealing a hole about a half inch wide in his upper back. I was surprised there wasn't more blood. In the movies, a red pool would be forming all around him, but this was more of a trickle.

Paco's friend ran to get his car while the rest of us gingerly grabbed Abel's arms, legs, and torso, lifting him up as carefully as we could. We hauled our injured leader into the back seat of the car, Paco and his friend on either side to support him. A few more climbed into the front seat of the car. I didn't go with them; I was scared. I had been in lots of fights, but no one had ever gotten shot before.

My whole body shook as I made my way home. Every noise made me jump. Every doorway held a potential threat. The sound of footsteps in the murky streets made my body tense, ready to fight whatever unknown entity lay in the shadows.

I hadn't been home long when I got the news Abel had died. I was convinced he had taken his last breath well before they had even reached the hospital. I punched the mattress on my bed, imagining it was the face of the man who had pulled the trigger.

"I'll get revenge, Abel." I swore into my pillow. But inwardly I knew that I was still too young and weak to do anything of the sort.

I slept fitfully, waking from nightmares that faded from memory the moment my eyes opened. When light finally filtered through the curtains of my room, banishing shadows, a sense of responsibility settled on me. I played through a thousand scenarios in my head. *If I had only done something. . . . Didn't I have a feeling that he had a gun? Could I have stopped him from shooting?*

I heard Mami moving around in the kitchen and remembered Abel's mother. Did she know her son wasn't coming home? Had anyone thought to tell her what had happened to her boy? She was probably still waiting for him, wondering where he was. As one of Abel's boys, it was my responsibility to tell her what had happened.

I dragged myself out of bed, pulled on my jeans, and tugged a sweater over my head. Every inch of me ached. *Abel is dead,* I reminded myself. I combed my hair back, swiped on some deodorant, and brushed my teeth. I should at least look presentable when I saw his mother.

I could hear her cries as I approached their house.

Someone must have already broken the news. I went in anyway, intent on paying my respects. I could see a small group gathered around Mrs. Ramirez. Through her tears she explained that she had been anticipating that something bad would happen to her son. She no longer had to worry about Abel being harmed or harming others. She didn't have to wonder where he was at night or if he was coming home.

I wanted to throw up. I knew Mami hated the crowd I was running with. I knew she worried about me too. What if my death were a relief to her? How many tears had she shed because of me? The problem was, I couldn't change now. I was in too deep.

Abel's death was in every paper at the corner store; the gory details of his death were splashed all over town. I grabbed a newspaper and started reading. He had internal bleeding, the article said. That explained why there was only a trickle of blood.

My eyes scanned the page, but my mind could only take in a few scattered words, like "gang leader." Those words were weak. He wasn't just some average joe with a few followers; Abel was the best. But the newspaper didn't paint him that way.

They didn't tell about how he took care of his boys or how incredibly cool he was. They talked about Abel and the Renegade Demons like we were characters in a soap opera. But they didn't know us. For as much information as they had gotten right, there was an equal amount that was wrong.

A car backfired outside and I jumped, my mind immediately back in the schoolyard with the sound of the gun shattering the quiet night. The image of Abel convulsing as he fell to the ground was as vivid as the moment it happened. I wished I could scrub it from my consciousness, but at the same time, I was glad I had that last memory of us—sitting on the steps together, talking about girls, and sharing a laugh.

For a few days I stayed closer to home, appalled that people were acting as if nothing had happened. The neighborhood crew still made trips to the corner store to buy cigarettes. Friends still stopped by our garage to lift weights with my older brothers and gossip about life. Mosquito still needed to be walked, and the garbage still needed to be taken out.

Elvis, Ruben, and Cid stopped by to commiserate and invited me to join them in the alley. It felt good. Like it used to before. . . .

Slowly, flashbacks from the night Abel died faded, and I managed to shove the fear of death from my mind. Before I realized what had happened, life was back to normal.

It was only a few weeks later that I met with a couple of coke dealers who offered me a piece of their action. I needed cash to fuel my habit, and if I started dealing, they assured me, I could make more money than I spent. In fact, if I was a good seller, I could be rich. I knew guys who paid with wads of cash and walked around in brand-name clothes. That could be me. I could be the guy with the pimped-out ride—not that I was old enough to drive.

I started small, not willing to risk getting caught with a big stash on me. I already had a pretty good network. I knew who was using and what they could afford. In no time, I was raking in $200, even $300, a week.

I got good at reading people. I could tell if someone was coming to buy or if they just wanted to shoot the breeze, even from across the street. One day this guy approached me, and I could tell just from the way he walked that he was looking for coke.

"Herman, right? I'm lookin' for an eight ball." His eyes darted around, and he shuffled his feet nervously. He seemed like a newbie but a big spender.

An eight ball is three and a half grams. It was a lot of dough. I liked clients like this. I fished in my pocket and took out the eight ball. I had no sooner placed it in his hands than the little punk took off running.

I tore after him, shouting curses at his back. I'd almost reached him when he jumped into his car. I dove in after him.

He didn't even fumble as he cranked the key in the ignition and yanked the gearshift into drive. I felt my weight shift and was almost thrown from the vehicle onto the street. But with one hand I gripped the rim of the door, and with the other I held tightly to his shirt collar. There was no thought in my mind but to stop him and take back what was mine.

"Stop the car! Stop the car!" I screamed.

The car careened wildly down the narrow streets; he wasn't going to stop. It would be a miracle if we didn't smash into one of the boxy sedans parked on either side. That eight ball mocked me from the pocket of his jeans. I released his collar and stretched my hand across his side, my face millimeters from his. There was panic in his eyes, but he was in a much safer position than I was. Gravity pulled at me. The muscles in my arms began to tremble, and my fingers ached. I'd be thrown under the car if I didn't jump. I let go and pushed with my legs, clearing the door and tumbling onto the road.

The pavement clawed at my skin as I hit the ground . . . but I was alive.

I got to my feet and brushed myself off. The blood roaring through my veins and dripping from my cuts was a sign that I was as tough and as cool as anyone you could possibly meet on the streets of New York. Or so I thought.

A few days later, I stopped in at one of the houses I used for selling. It was close to home—104th Street and 38th Avenue. One of the other dealers, Raul, pulled out a little bag and handed it to me. Raul was quite a bit older than me. He was easily edging in on thirty. He had a Puerto Rican accent, so I never bothered to ask where he was from. He was short too. I was already taller than he was, but what really made Raul stand out was his nose; it was bulbous, with a large birthmark. I couldn't help but think that when he snorted drugs, they had an easy run up to his brain.

The packet he had handed me was folded into three sections. "Dark brown, with a stamp on it," he informed me.

"Dark brown with a stamp" was a particular type of heroin. He took out a dollar bill and poured the molasses-colored powder onto it. Then he took a business card and scraped some onto the palm of my hand. Without a thought, I put it up to my nose and inhaled quickly.

It went straight to my brain. The high was so fast . . . and so high. I was hooked. It was like everything had accelerated and slowed down, as if I were in control of time itself. All my senses seemed heightened. I could hear the sound of sirens miles away and still notice the ticking of a clock and the rushing of blood through my veins. I could smell exhaust from cars outside and the vaguely sour smell of rotting garbage in the kitchen.

A stash house on 104th full of rented rooms became one of our main hangouts. One of the rooms belonged to a guy we called Cuba, so nicknamed for his citizenship. I'd known him a long time, longer than I'd known Jayson and at least as long as I had known Cid and Elvis.

One day, Cuba brought a girl back to the house. I was in the bathroom, a line of heroin on the laminate counter in front of me and a massive claw-foot tub behind me where I could lie down afterward. The girl walked right in as if she didn't see me and pulled a long rubber band out of the pocket of her jeans. She was older than me, early twenties maybe, but world weary. Her skin was dull, her eyes lifeless, and her straw-like hair hung limply around her emaciated face.

Once she'd pulled the band tightly around her scabby arm, she pulled out a spoon and cooked up some heroin. She filled the needle and prodded around for a vein, smiling when she found one. I felt my stomach clench and a shiver run through me as the needle pierced her skin, delivering the drug right into her bloodstream. Her reaction was immediate.

She looked dead. She was so still, sitting on the floor. I couldn't tell if she was breathing. It freaked me out, but I couldn't look away. The drugs were already messing with my mind, but seeing her there, a shell of a person, did something to me.

I promised myself, *I will never get to the point where I have to inject it into my veins like that. Never.*

Her high wore off quicker than my own. When it did, she started scratching at her arms, tearing at the skin, looking to reclaim even a droplet of the drug from her veins.

I left the stash house mumbling, "That will never be me. That will never be me."

But it could be. No matter what I tried to tell myself, I was already an addict.

It wasn't long before I needed another fix. I wasn't far from a local video store. The owner was a guy from the neighborhood who used to sell us weed, so it seemed like a safe place to do a line or two of coke. In fact, I had some heroin on me too. I could try a speedball.

I wound my way through the aisles of VHS tapes and pushed through the door of the bathroom, locking it behind me. I sniffed the coke first and then cut up the heroin.

Within seconds of sniffing the brown powder, I started to feel sick. My head spun. The floor underneath me moved up and down, up and down. My cheeks felt numb and saliva filled my mouth; I began to vomit. I retched violently, as if my gut wanted to push its way out through my esophagus. Adrenaline pulsed through me. I needed to run. I would tear out of there and run for miles if the vomiting would just stop.

And then as suddenly as the burst of adrenaline came, it vanished. I sank to the ground, my muscles like limp rags. I wanted to get out of there, but I couldn't get to my feet. It was as if an unknown force pinned me down. I couldn't even lift my head from the floor. *If I somehow survive this, I will never touch heroin or coke again*, I promised whatever higher power might be listening.

I don't know how long I lay on that sticky tiled floor, but eventually my strength returned and I was able to stand. I stumbled out of the store and went home to bed, lucky to be alive.

––––––––

"Hey, Herman." Cuba called me up a few days later. "You should come see *Purple Rain* wit' us. It's gonna be a blast, man. You'll love it."

At the theater later, we found our seats. As the lights dimmed, Cuba handed me a little stamp-sized piece of paper. "It's way better with acid, man."

I hadn't promised to stop doing drugs altogether, just coke and heroin. Without an ounce of guilt, I popped the paper acid as the opening credits rolled. In seconds I was tripping hard. It felt like the whole movie theater was moving. My heart started racing, and my legs started to twitch. A part of me knew that the guys on the screen were not really a part of my world, but I was sure that there was a real threat. Somewhere beyond my vision, the vile masses were out to get me. I leaned across to Cuba.

"Man, I gotta split. I need to go home."

I didn't wait for a response. I stumbled over a few pairs of legs, falling into the aisle. I got up and sprinted up the ramp toward the door. The floor seemed to move beneath me, and I could hear the pounding of footsteps behind me. In my time as a gang member I had racked up a few enemies. I could be shot or stabbed if I was caught by whoever was chasing me.

I was panting hard by the time I ran up the stairs to my front door. My mami called out to me as I passed through the hall, "¿Herman? Estás en casa temprano. You're home early, what hap—"

I didn't answer. I didn't stop until I was back in the bedroom I shared with my brother Emilio. I shut the door behind me and climbed onto my bed.

Emilio took one look at my wide eyes and heavy breathing and knew I was tripping. "Whoa, Herman . . . what did you take?"

The whole room seemed to be shaking, like an earthquake had targeted our house. I grabbed on to my blankets, trying to hold myself steady. "Purple head acid. . . . I'm trippin', man."

Emilio sat beside me, put his arm around my shoulder, and tried to talk me through it. I was grateful to him. That's what brothers are for, right? When it was finally over and I calmed down, I lay back in bed and stared at the ceiling. I had to lay off acid altogether—tripping was not my thing. I felt like it was taking control of me, and I didn't like it.

4

A Change of Scene

They caught me.

But not with drugs as most of my friends would have expected. I was arrested and convicted of grand larceny. I didn't think it was as "grand" as the cops were trying to make it out to be. I'd only stolen a car radio. Still, it was enough to get me sent to juvie.

Spofford, a juvenile detention center in the Bronx, was a holding tank for young offenders. At fourteen, I thought my time with the gangs and selling drugs had made me hard, fearless even. But as we drove through the gates of this concrete garrison, a new kind of fear awakened in me. I felt vulnerable . . . exposed. In here, I had no big brothers I could call on to back me up. No Mami to rub my hands and kiss my cheek when my world felt out of control. No Papi to offer me advice and make me feel like I was bigger and stronger than other guys.

The driver pulled through the smaller gate into a cavernous room. This place was built for hard-core criminals, not kids. A uniformed officer escorted me from the van, locking a restraint around my waist while another officer handcuffed me to it.

"Follow me," the taller of the two guards instructed.

The booking process was efficient. I was fingerprinted, pictures were taken, and I was handed an identification card before being ushered into a warehouse of sorts.

"Herman Mendoza?" a dry voice called me forward. They removed my belt and shoes, then handed me some brown institutional slippers. The slippers weren't too bad. They were better than walking barefoot on the cold, dusty, concrete floor.

The officer who escorted me from the van motioned me forward again. "Follow me to your dorm."

"Dorm" was a nice name for "roach-infested cell." I sat down on the creaky cot and tried to hold back tears. They kept calling it a juvenile detention center, but it was jail, pure and simple. The only reminder of the world outside was a sliver of a window looking out on a dismal street miles out of reach.

Loneliness washed over me. I hadn't realized that loneliness could feel like an actual ache. An image of Mami crying at the kitchen table sprang to mind unbidden. Tears pooled in my own eyes. My older brothers—Gabriel, Emilio, Fabian, and Dante—were probably tiptoeing around the house, cursing my stupidity and trying not to cause her any more trouble today. But would any of them try to comfort her? Papi couldn't. He'd still be at work. No matter what was happening, he was never able to come home until the weekend.

New fears came to my mind. Would my family treat me the same when I got out? Would I be ostracized?

I shivered in the dark room. It had been like a hothouse when I arrived, but as soon as the sun went down the room cooled. I tried to cover as much of myself as I could with the thin blanket and go to sleep. There were strange creaks and constant scratching sounds, the audible evidence of rats, but that was nothing compared to the constant jabbering of the other guys in the dorm. Every few minutes someone shouted, "Everyone just shut up!" Which was quickly followed by, "You shut up." Which led to a round of expletives and name calling.

It was hours before I slipped into unconsciousness, the vision of rats nibbling at my toes haunting my dreams.

When morning finally came, I was rounded up with the others and led to the cafeteria. I didn't expect the food to be good, but it was worse than I'd imagined. Things that should be solid were runny, and things that should be liquid had clumps. It was cold and unappetizing, but I was hungry enough to eat anyway.

The cafeteria in juvie had a social hierarchy that would put any high school lunchroom to shame. Everywhere I looked, I saw something that shocked me. Beside me sat a really small kid. He looked like he was barely out of diapers. *What on earth could he have done to land himself here?* I wondered.

Just beyond him was a guy I would have sworn was closing in on twenty-five. No terrible teenage moustache for him. He was sporting a five-o'clock shadow at nine in the morning.

I was the youngest and smallest in the gang when I ran with the Renegade Demons, but I never felt like I couldn't hold my own. The guys in Spofford were different. If I didn't want to be a constant whipping post for the Goliaths who called this place home, I was going to have to fight.

Three days later I made the mistake of glancing up as I passed one of the big guys in the hall. He grabbed my shoulder and spun me around.

"What you looking at?!"

"N-nothing," I mumbled. Keeping my eyes trained on my brown slippers, I tried to pull away. Another mistake.

He swore under his breath. "Looks like you want to play the bathroom."

I'd heard the expression before; it was enough to make my blood run cold. To "play the bathroom" was a challenge to fight. It was one of the only places where the correction officers couldn't see us. I was terrified, but I tried my best to appear calm.

I led the way to the restroom; five guys followed. Not good. These guys could kill me. If I wanted to survive we'd have to fight here, near some officers and where there was at least a chance I could be saved. I balled my hand into a fist and took a swing at the guy closest to me, making sure to put all my weight behind it.

The surprise attack only worked in my favor for a few seconds. Their fists started flying, hard and fast. I tucked my elbows in, raised my fists to block the punches to my face, and dropped into a squat. There were too many of them and there was no one to back me up.

We were only a short run from the correction officer's station. If I could make it there, I could take cover underneath the desk.

I scrambled forward and crawled low. In a panic, the officer there called for backup. A rush of officers in riot gear flooded the housing unit. In minutes they'd restrained and removed my attackers.

I was still conscious when a few officers rushed me to the infirmary, laying me on a paper-covered bed. Blood soaked the paper before the nurse had a chance to clean my wounds. She handed me some ibuprofen and a paper cup with water. It was hard to swallow, but the cool water helped ease the burning in my lungs. The cold packs helped even more, but I knew that the black eyes and swollen lips would take some time to heal.

Mami came a few days later. I missed her more than I wanted to admit. I knew she wouldn't like to see me in such rough shape, but my heart broke when I walked in and she started sobbing. "¡Mi hijo!" she wailed.

I instinctively put a hand to my face. It was still swollen, and although I had no mirror to assess the damage, I knew it was bad. There were not enough ice packs or Band-Aids in the world to hide what had been done to me.

We cried together. She held my hands, kissing the bruised knuckles and wetting them with her tears. But there was no sense of comfort when our visit ended. Instead, guilt took up residence in the pit of my stomach. I had made Mami cry . . . just like Abel's mother had cried.

It was six months before I was released. Three months in Spofford and another three in a slightly better center upstate.

I was surprisingly nervous to go home when the time came. I had no idea what kind of welcome I could expect. It wasn't like I was returning as a hero from the battlefield, although it felt a bit like that to me. But walking through the doors, breathing in the familiar scent of my home, I knew that whatever demands or rules Mami and Papi might place on me now, it would be better than spending one more minute in juvie.

"Herman, ¡tengo una sorpresa para ti!" Mami called from the front door.

I was curious what kind of surprise she had prepared. She sounded excited. I'd expected her to really crack down on me when I returned. I'd prepared myself for all sorts of restrictions, but it had been almost two weeks, and she hadn't really said much about any rules.

"¡Vamos a comprar una bicicleta!" Mami said, a big smile on her face.

Now she was getting me a bicycle? She must have really missed me. I grabbed my stuff and headed out the door with her.

Emilio was standing beside our old blue Pontiac, spinning the car keys on his finger. I jumped in the car, impatient to get going. I was going to look so cool, riding around the neighborhood on my very own bicycle. I didn't even care what color or make it was. The guys in my class would be envious, and the girls would all want to ride with me.

Mami chatted happily as we drove along, but I could barely focus on what she was saying. *A bicycle of my own!* That's all my mind had room for.

I smiled out the side window as Corona's familiar landmarks passed us by. It wasn't until we had turned off onto Grand Central Parkway, heading toward JFK Airport, that I suspected something was up. Mami kept asking questions, switching from topic to topic without waiting for answers. Then she would stop midsentence and stare into space for minutes at a time.

"Mami, ¿a dónde vamos? Where are we going?"

Emilio glanced over at Mami. She sighed and glanced back at me. *What was that about?*

"Herman, tú sabes que quiero una vida mejor para ti." She tried to keep the enthusiasm in her voice as she told me she wanted a better life for me, but her voice broke more than once. I didn't quite understand what she was talking about.

"Te vas a quedar con tu abuela y abuelo."

My mind couldn't make sense of it. She wanted me to stay with my grandparents. "Are you sending me to D.R.?"

Emilio, who had been silent until then, picked up the explanation when Mami broke down. "Mami's worried about you. Abuelo and Abuela are expecting you. You can get a fresh start there. . . . We'll send you a bicycle. We weren't lying about getting you a bike."

He glanced in the rearview mirror, trying to read my face. My brain could barely process what I was hearing. Mami had lied to me!

It was a half minute longer before I remembered I had nothing with me but my backpack. "I'm not even packed!"

"Mami packed your things already." Emilio's voice was assertive. "They're in the trunk."

I had always loved our family trips to the Dominican Republic, but I wasn't sure I wanted to live there. And to make matters worse, I would be away from home again. I remembered how lonely I had felt in Spofford, leaving behind my gang, my friends, my brothers, and Mami.

I shook my head to clear it. I was being silly. I would be staying in a room at my grandparents' home. It was a far cry from that minuscule, rat-infested cell.

I thought I knew what to expect when we landed in Las Américas Airport in Santo Domingo, but I had forgotten that the Dominican Republic felt a lot like a sauna this time of year. It felt good for a few minutes, but soon sweat was dripping down my face and running down my spine.

"¡Herman, muchacho!" My grandparents welcomed me with open arms, kissing my cheeks.

Abuela reminded me that the drive to their place was a long one, and if I needed anything, I should tell her before we went. I quickly went to the bathroom while they bought me a cold drink for the road.

A lot had been built up around the airport since the last time I was there. When I had come with my family in previous summers, it had seemed like such a quiet little place. But now in 1984, it was crowded with people, and a new highway ran heavy with traffic.

We arrived at my grandparents' hometown of Bonao in the province of Monseñor Nouel. Buela—that is what I called my grandmother—helped me settle into my new room. I liked it. Its big, shuttered window, unlike the window in my bedroom back home, could open onto the green grass and fruit trees in the yard.

"Your cousins are excited to see you," Buela said, helping me find a place for my socks and underwear.

I was excited to see them too; we had always gotten along. As punishments go, this one was shaping up to be pretty great.

"Y, tu madre hizo arreglos para que fueras a la escuela." She explained that my mother had arranged with Colegio San Pablo, a private school in Bonao, to let me take an entrance exam even though the school year was well under way.

"No hay problema," I said, confident I would ace the test.

I was wrong.

"Ay, Herman. Tch, tch, tch," Buela tutted when we received the results.

I groaned in response. The school was going to put me back a grade. I would be the oldest and biggest kid on the school bus. Not cool.

The previous year, I'd had my own business, albeit an illegal one. I'd made more money in twelve months than most Dominicans could dream of, and now I was stuck with a bunch of little kids, learning stuff I'd learned before. It was humiliating.

"¡Herman, vamonos!" Abuelo called from the front porch. He had on the sombrero he always wore when he left the house. Not the Mexican-style hat made famous by Speedy Gonzales, but a 1950s *el campesino*, a straw fedora with a flat brim. My grandfather wasn't a tall man, maybe five foot seven, but there was something striking about his presence. If Humphrey Bogart were Dominican, he'd probably have fashioned himself after my abuelo.

When businesspeople came to the house to visit him, they always called him Don Pancho. The way they said it made me think it must be a term of respect. I later found out that Pancho was just an abbreviation of his first name, Francisco. Still, from where I was standing, he was one of the greatest men I knew.

I stuffed my wallet in the back of my jeans and grabbed a baseball cap. Abuelo was straddling his motorcycle, waiting for me. I climbed up behind him, and we hit the road. The breeze swirled around my face, taking the edge off the beating sun.

"Where we headed?" I asked in my accented Spanish.

"A trabajar," he shouted back, his words almost lost in our wake.

I liked joining him for work. We toured the fields and outbuildings And checked in with his workers. I watched as he gave commands and made suggestions where necessary. Abuelo wasn't a highly educated man, but he was a hard worker with a lot of knowledge in the agriculture business.

When we arrived home for dinner at the end of the day, I had a feeling I hadn't experienced in a long time. In fact, I didn't quite know what to name it.

After we ate, we all found spots on the porch. Abuelo in his swing, rocking and smoking his pipe. Buela nearby, peeling fruit for us. Every so often Abuelo pulled his pipe from between his lips to tell me a joke. His weren't the usual grandfather jokes—he was really funny. I wiped tears from my eyes, I was laughing so hard.

The sun set earlier on the island than it did in New York. When I went to bed that night, I thought of my family. Like I had done in Spoffsord, I imagined what they might be doing, but this time there was no accompanying loneliness. It may not have been an exciting day, but it was a good day.

Contentment. That was the feeling I hadn't been able to name. I was content here.

5

Old Habits Die Hard

Life in Bonao was simple. Most days were spent on trips with Buela to the market or to Abeulo's plantation, with me learning the business as he went about his day. They invited me into their lives without criticism or mention of the life I had left behind in Corona. I felt loved and accepted. Buela, especially, was kind and gentle. Her strong Catholic beliefs made her live a strict and conservative life, but she never pushed me to abide by the same rules she did.

I had only one real complaint about life in the Dominican Republic. School was boring.

The classrooms were stuffy, and I wasn't learning anything new. To get through the long, tedious days, I found myself a new gang. Not a literal gang—just the kids who were up to no good. Kids who knew where the parties were and didn't always feel the need to adhere to the law.

"Hey, Herman. ¿Quieres ir con nosotros al club? Wanna come with us to the club?" one of my new friends asked as we walked home from school.

I grinned. "Sí, claro." Of course I did. "But where do I get an ID?" These kids must have connections.

They laughed. "ID? Who's gonna ask?"

My eyes widened. I could go to a club, and no one would ask for my identification or tell me I was too young to be there? I was in!

Our club of choice blasted salsa music, and a disco ball shone shards of light on patrons in various states of inebriation. My stomach clenched as I followed my friends to the bar, and my voice shook a little as I asked for a beer. Without questions, the bartender pulled a beer, handing it to me in a tall glass. I grabbed it as if it might disappear, gulping it down as I walked to a table. It was cool and refreshing, and I wanted another.

I wasn't completely wasted when I walked back to my grandparents' place that evening, but I was far from sober. If I turned my head, the room took an extra second to catch up with my vision. I noticed my abuelo was still sitting on the porch smoking his pipe.

He motioned for me to join him. I sat down in the chair beside him and attempted to look normal. He took another drag on his pipe, and a little circle of red appeared in the dark, followed by a little gray puff of smoke. He looked at me with a sort of lazy contemplation, and I felt my shoulders tighten. Did he guess that I was drunk?

He started to tell me a story. It was a solid minute before I realized it was a joke and not a life lesson he was trying to relate. I sank back in relief. I listened and laughed the way we usually did. His story reminded me of a Dominican song that was everywhere at the time. It was full of double entendres, and feeling a little bolder than usual, I sang it, replacing the names in the song with his and Buela's.

I sang about how tough and mean he was and how he needed some loving from his wife. He burst out laughing.

Despite Buela's long skirts and high-necked blouses, they'd had thirteen children together. There must have been plenty of loving in their marriage.

Abuelo, in hysterics, almost fell off the rocking chair.

The image of my conservative grandmother being romanced by my grandfather—it was too much. I was laughing so hard I could barely finish the song.

I studied Abuelo through my tears. I loved this old man. Moments like these made me want to be a better person. Someone he and Buela would be proud of. At the very least, I could be a little smarter about who I ran with and what state I returned home in.

I wanted to be better, but it seemed like trouble found me.

I went out with my cousin, looking for something fun to do, when a riot broke out. Forty or so people had gathered in the street to protest the high rate of inflation. Tires were rolled into a pile and set ablaze. "¡Abuso! ¡Corrupción! Abuse! Corruption!" the crowd chanted.

It looked like fun, and it didn't involve any of my usual foibles. *What would be the harm in joining in?* A delicious feeling of joy and adrenaline fluttered in my stomach as I shouted with the people, fists raised in the air against the government. My cousin and I cheered as men poured gasoline over another pile of tires and threw a match.

Suddenly, the military shot bullets in the air and threw tear gas into the crowd. People were getting hurt. Some of the rioters picked rocks off the side of the road and threw them at the advancing unit of soldiers, who fought back forcefully.

For a moment, my cousin and I stood rooted to the spot, dumbfounded. If we didn't run, we could be arrested, possibly even killed!

We took off, legs pumping hard, feet barely touching the ground. I don't know if it was the tear gas in the air or just the exertion, but my lungs burned.

My aunt's house was the closest safe place we could think of. We made a beeline for it. The front door barely slowed us down as we barreled inside and down the hall to the nearest bedroom. We locked the door and crawled under the bed, panting and wiping away sweat. Even that didn't feel safe enough. We lay there for hours, silently waiting for the riot to end.

It wasn't until we heard the streets grow quiet and people moving around the house that we crawled out from under the bed. I'd almost forgotten what it was like to have that rush of adrenaline. I'd forgotten how addictive it could be.

I didn't want to go back to school on Monday. "Abuelo, pleeease!" I begged. "I will help you every day at the plantation. I'll do whatever you need me to do."

"No, no, no, Herman. You must stay in school. Your Spanish is getting better every day," my abuelo assured me.

"But I'm just repeating things I already know. I'm not really getting an education."

I knew the real reason they wanted me to be in school: School was my babysitter. The teachers would watch out for me and make sure I didn't have a chance to get into trouble. My grandparents couldn't do that for me twenty-four hours a day. I wouldn't win this one; I would have to find another way.

By the next Monday, I just couldn't stand it anymore. I climbed on the bus as usual, and Buela waved good-bye. I waited until the teacher had taken attendance, then found an excuse to leave the classroom. The building was in a protected compound, and the only way out was over the wall.

I walked along the wall until I found a spot concealed by a tree. I jumped up, grabbed hold of the top of the wall, and pulled myself up. I was almost over when I heard a voice behind me.

"Herman Mendoza. Ven conmigo a la oficina."

I was forced to climb back down and report to the office. To my delight, my little stunt was enough to warrant expulsion. Buela's look of disappointment when she arrived made me feel bad, but not bad enough to eclipse my joy.

"Tomorrow, you'll come to work with me," Abuelo informed me.

I nodded solemnly, but I was excited. Abuelo rivaled Abel Ramirez in the cool department. When he went to work, it was with a machete strapped to his left side and a .38-caliber pistol on his right. And he knew how to use them. Most landowners who worked the fields were armed to keep intruders and thieves away.

But despite the positive turn of events, I still felt a little bored. A fifteen-year-old can only spend so much time with senior citizens before boredom sets in, no matter how much he loves them. Fortunately, my expulsion from school hadn't lost me any friendships.

———

I was out riding my new bicycle one morning when I spotted Carmen Salcedo walking with another girl. Carmen and I had been in the same class back in New York.

"Carmen! What are you doing here? When did you arrive?"

She was as shocked as I was to see a familiar face. "I'm living here for a bit with family. You know my best friend, Alexandra."

I heard Carmen talking, but I had trouble tearing my eyes away from her friend. Alexandra's dark eyes were captivating. I could feel my hands get clammy and my heart rate increase.

The pretty girl smiled. "I remember you. We were in school together."

"Yeah. I remember you."

After Carmen filled me in on news from home, we both hesitated, not eager to say good-bye.

"Now that I know you're here, we can hang out," Carmen said. "In fact, Alexandra is throwing a quinceañera for me this Saturday. You should come." She wrote down the address. It was only a few blocks from my grandparents' house.

I knew Carmen's sweet fifteen birthday party would be legendary. More than that, it was going to be packed with girls my age. How could I refuse?

———

I could hear the pulsing rhythm of the merengue before I even got close to the house. I ran a hand over my short hair before walking through the gates and then wormed my way through the throng of partygoers to Carmen. Carmen was standing beside her pretty friend Alexandra, whom I immediately struck up a conversation with about school in Queens. She giggled and said, "Everyone in school knew the Mendoza brothers. I was in Dante's class."

We talked about New York, and I did my best to impress her with stories. I knew talking about the gangs or the drugs would be a turnoff. But there was a time, just before I had joined the

Renegade Demons, that I had made a name for myself as a break-dancer. "They called me A-Rocker. A. R. for short."

I really missed those days. I told her how I used to go down to Flushing Meadows Park and USA Jackson Heights Roller Rink to compete. Grandmaster Flash, Run DMC, and Kool Moe Dee would meet there and throw down some epic rap battles. Hip-hop wasn't recognized in the mainstream yet; it was straight up inner-city culture. They would take out a boom box, a couple of turntables, eight-tracks, and a cassette or two, and a crowd would gather.

"Do you want to see me bust a move?" I asked her.

I wasn't feeling nervous anymore. Alexandra had been smiling and talking with me for a solid twenty minutes. In party time, that was hours.

"Sure." She smiled again, eyes twinkling.

This was it. This was where I could shine. I walked with her to the dance floor and found a little spot. I made some space in the crowd and started with headspins and hand glides. Then I moved into some handstands and back spins. All my best moves.

She laughed and clapped, and the crowd that had gathered around clapped too. She and I talked about hanging out later. And I walked away feeling pretty good about life in the República Dominicana.

Unbeknown to me, back at the house, my grandparents had been discussing what to do with me. My late nights out with friends, coming home drunk, expulsion—it was too much. They couldn't do it anymore. The next morning, they called me into the kitchen and sat me down for a talk.

"It's time to go home, Herman. We can't take care of you if you don't ever listen to us," my grandfather said sternly.

I was a little conflicted as they told me about my departure, which was just a few months away, but not as much as I expected. As much as I enjoyed the beauty of the Dominican Republic and living with my grandparents, I missed the fast pace of city life. I was ready to go home.

6

BACK IN THE BIG APPLE

"Herman, ¡bienvenido a casa!"

My mother's words were welcoming, but she hesitated as she pulled me into her arms and kissed my cheeks. Something felt . . . off. Everything about my homecoming felt different than I had expected. The city seemed different, almost unfamiliar. My family was distant, as if we had lost the camaraderie we once enjoyed.

I had spent time in one of the most notorious juvenile detention centers in the United States. I had been exiled to the Dominican Republic, where I had two people to love me and watch over me every day. But I still sought out trouble.

"Lávate las manos y ven a comer algo."

Mami instructed me to wash up and come for dinner. Her face was unreadable. Was she even a little happy I was home? I nodded and carried my bags to my room. I slumped onto my bed and then stared at the ceiling for a few minutes before pulling myself up with a sigh and heading for the washroom.

I peeled my clothes off and jumped into the shower. The warm water ran over my face and down my back, erasing the smell of the Dominican Republic from my skin. I was surprised to discover that within hours of being back, D.R. felt like a memory.

I toweled off, dressed, and joined my whole family at the table. The worry in Mami's eyes as she placed my favorite dishes on the table made me want to reform. For her, I could set myself on a different course. Someday I would make her proud. I sat down at the dining table with a smile on my face.

My friends gave me a warmer welcome than my family had. They gathered around, slapping me on the back and shaking my hand with our old secret handshake. "We missed you, man!"

I grinned and couldn't help but hold my head a little higher. We walked down the streets of Corona like we owned them. This was my turf, and these were my people.

Jayson pulled me aside later and fished a little package from his pocket. Coke. My heart started to pound. I should resist. I made a show of feeling my pockets for money I knew I didn't have.

"I got nothing on me, man."

His chuckle was more of a snort. "No problem. It's on me. Let's go."

I wavered.

He flapped the packet in front of me before turning and heading for a friend's place. *Mami won't know. I won't go home while I'm stoned.*

I waited for the familiar rush of euphoria. It didn't come. I felt a little off, and it wasn't a good feeling. I flopped back on a chair and waited for my head to clear. *I'm never trying drugs again. It isn't worth it,* I promised myself.

I walked out of that house and never looked back. I didn't realize that as I walked down Thirty-Seventh Avenue I was being watched. If I had turned my head, I might have seen Alexandra watching as I sauntered down the street with a slight "thug" hitch in my step and trying to remember where she'd seen me. I might have seen the sadness in her eyes as she remembered who I was and turned away, disappointed in the life I had chosen.

Me during my gang days

7

Four Funerals
and a Brush-Off

Nineteen eighty-six was the summer of funerals. I don't know what it was about those few months back in Queens, but they had more than their fair share of grief. Several of the funerals were gang related. Stabbings. Shootings. I went to a few of them out of respect. But the funeral Mami forced me to go to was different. It was for a young woman who Mami kept calling my cousin, but we were only distantly related.

I was the last to get ready, and Mami was impatient. "¡Herman! ¡Date rápido!"

I was only going to please my mother, and that meant I had to wear a starched collar and long-sleeved shirt. I pulled on some pleated jeans and tucked the uncomfortable button-up shirt inside. The funeral parlor didn't have AC, and I wasn't too keen on sweating in the packed room, but the reformed Herman sometimes had to do things he didn't want to do.

As soon as we got inside, Mami, my brothers, and I separated. Mami had people she wanted to talk to. My brothers had friends there who demanded their attention.

I looked around the room at the mourners. I noticed familiar people, but one exquisite face stood out. She was incredibly attractive, and I felt like I had seen her before.

I found my way to her side, still trying to place where I knew her from. I held up my hand in a lame imitation of a wave. "Hello."

She smiled, her eyes twinkled, and my heart caught in my chest.

"Did you . . . know . . ." Words kept getting stuck on my tongue. I nodded toward the pictures of the deceased.

Sadness crept into her eyes. "She was a very close friend."

Poor girl. I thought of Abel and how, even now, I grieved for him. I didn't have much to say, but I wanted to keep talking. I tried the usual run-of-the-mill funeral chatter, but even as I asked how the family were doing, my eyes were asking her something else entirely.

As she answered my question, I was sure her eyes were telling me she was interested too.

Emilio found me just then. "We're heading home." It wasn't information; it was a demand.

I made my apologies. "I hope we run into each other again sometime."

She nodded sweetly and waved good-bye.

I didn't realize until Emilio and I were almost home that I hadn't asked for her name. I kicked myself. How was I supposed to ask around about her if I didn't even know her name?

A month passed, and with the rising August heat, tempers flared on the streets. It wasn't long before we heard that another young guy from our neighborhood had been killed.

As I dressed for the funeral, I wondered if I would see that girl again. Just in case, I pulled on a muscle shirt and jeans. I had been working out with my older brothers in the garage and had gotten pretty ripped. I flexed in front of the mirror.

I saw her the minute I walked through the doors of the funeral parlor. She had on a summer dress, soft and light. It wasn't figure hugging. It wasn't too short or too low-cut. She didn't need to dress like that to turn heads; she had a body that could stop traffic.

I found my way to her. My first order of business was finding out her name. She almost laughed when I asked.

"It's Alexandra," she said. "We met at Carmen's quinceañera. You don't remember?"

Scenes from Carmen's party in the Dominican Republic came flooding back. I had spent the entire night trying to impress her, and somehow I had forgotten her name? I was an idiot.

In my defense, when you see someone out of context, the mind has a hard time putting two and two together. At least that was my excuse.

"It must be destiny," I joked.

She raised an eyebrow. "Destiny?"

"That life keeps placing us in each other's paths."

She giggled, but I was serious. "Maybe it's divine intervention?"

She swatted my arm, and my muscle flexed under her hand. Oh yes, the muscle shirt had been a good choice.

"Carmen's party wasn't the first time we met, you know," Alexandra said. "I used to see you taking the bus to school. It would pass right in front of my mom's house. It was hard to miss you sitting in the very back." Her voice was teasing. "And then you came to my house a few times after the party in D.R. Did you forget that too?"

Man, I had a bad memory.

She looked at me and smiled. I wasn't sure it was flirtatious, but it was all the fuel my crush needed to burn hotter. "Will you be around later? Do you want to . . ."

She was shaking her head before I could finish my question. "Sorry, no. I have to get back home."

My heart sank. I knew a brush-off when I heard one. So much for destiny.

8

Mr. GQ

My sophomore year brought a new school: Newtown High in Elm-hurst, Queens. And since I had decided to turn my life around, I thought I might as well go for a new look too. No more gang apparel. I flipped through the pages of *GQ*, searching for just the right outfit.

The guys from *Miami Vice*, with their pastel shirts and Ray-Ban sunglasses, had the absolute coolest vibe. I didn't need the whole suit. A pastel green T-shirt with rolled-up sleeves tucked into a pair of pleated, white linen pants would do the trick. I looked through all my shoes. Sneakers. They wouldn't work. I would have to buy some penny loafers. And I could say good-bye to my socks. I wouldn't be needing those anymore.

A bigger issue was my hair. No one in the pages of *GQ* had my curly hair. Every single man wore theirs long, straight, and slicked back. If I wanted to look like Don Johnson, I would have to sneak away to the salon and get it straightened.

It turned out getting my hair straightened was painful. The chemicals burned my scalp, the smell made me gag, and it was pricey! But I looked good. I was going to walk into Newtown High School, and heads were going to turn.

I soon found out I wasn't the only guy in my class to have grown taller and broader. And the girls . . . they looked more like women than teenagers. I would have to start collecting numbers in my little black book.

Almost a month into the first semester, I saw a familiar face through the windows of a supermarket. Alexandra!

I stopped in my tracks. She was a cashier there. That meant I now knew where to find her. Mami was expecting me, but I had a few minutes and our house was only two blocks away. I pushed through the doors, hoping to catch her attention, but she wasn't looking. I fished in my pockets for some money and came up empty handed. The sun was already low, and I'd have to run if I didn't want Mami to worry.

I made another trip to the store that night, this time under the guise of buying something for Mami. By the time I got there my heart was pounding. I could see Alexandra at her register before I even went in. I took a deep, calming breath and pushed through the doors. She didn't look up.

I sauntered slowly down the aisles, picking up odds and ends and putting them back again. I didn't have a lot to get for Mami, but I wanted to calm down a bit before I went to pay.

I practiced what I would say to her. *"Oh hey, Alexandra. You work here?"*

Kind of lame.

"Hey, you're still around?"

Worse. Why would I try to sound disinterested?

I picked up some milk and bread, tossed a bag of coffee in my basket, and headed to the checkout line. Alexandra's line wasn't the shortest, but that gave me more time to plan my greeting.

When it was my turn, she smiled at me and waved me forward. "Herman!"

I walked up to the counter, plunked down my few items, swallowed hard, and with my best Don Johnson impression said, "Alexandra!"

She giggled. "What are you up to?"

I had no idea what to say in response. I really wanted to ask for her number; I didn't want to have to wait months again for another opportunity to talk to her. Should I just bite the bullet and ask her out? "Can I walk you home after work?" My stomach twisted.

She nodded. "Sure."

Yes! She said yes!

I walked out of the store with the same slow saunter I had affected when I entered, but as soon as I got past the windows I broke into a sprint. I was panting by the time I got home with the groceries. I dropped the bag on the kitchen table and headed for my room. I ran a comb through my hair and tucked my shirt back into my linen pants. I did a quick pit check and sprayed a little more cologne before rushing back to the store. It was almost closing time. I didn't want her to have to wait for me on the street.

"Hi," I said again as Alexandra came out of the store. My voice cracked a little, and I felt my face grow hot.

She smiled a little more shyly than usual.

"This way?" I realized I didn't know where she lived.

She pointed in the opposite direction. I followed her for the first few steps until she turned and waited for me to catch up. Somehow that eased my nerves, and we talked comfortably the rest of the way.

I made a habit of shopping at her store. Some days I would make multiple trips, buying one item at a time so I would have more excuses to go through her checkout, and I walked her home to her sister's house as often as she'd let me.

Her niece worked at the store too, and I caught them whispering one day. Giselda was a nice kid, but there was mischief in her eyes as she looked my way. Alexandra glanced at me and blushed.

That night, Giselda joined us on the walk to Alexandra's place, further hampering my flirt game. When we got to her place, I asked if she could stay out. "Maybe we could go for a walk?"

My hands started to feel clammy. If she said yes I was going to confess how I felt and ask her to be my girlfriend. I could see she was debating something in her head, and I gave her a minute.

"If I don't go home, my sister is going to suspect I am sneaking around with someone . . . but maybe if I offer to take my baby niece Lucy out, it would be okay."

I wasn't thrilled with the idea, but it was better than a concrete no.

I waited while she was inside, growing nervous that she wouldn't return. She came out several minutes later with her two-year-old niece strapped into a stroller.

We came to a park and sat down. Alexandra parked the stroller beside us and handed her niece a rattle. The little girl was half asleep, but she grabbed it in her pudgy hand and shook it a few times.

"What was it that your niece Giselda said to you earlier? It looked like it was about me." I turned so I could see Alexandra's face and those eyes—they were like black pearls behind long lashes.

A blush pinked her cheeks. She practically glowed in the last rays of the evening sun. "She said she thought you liked me, because you keep coming into the store and you're always looking at me."

"Whatever gave her that idea?" I laughed and gave her a wink.

Alexandra's flush deepened, and she looked at her little niece. Everything she said and did enthralled me. I had a sudden compulsion to keep her talking.

"What do you want to do when you finish school?" I asked.

She seemed surprised by the change in topic and took a second to think. When she did speak, my eyes were drawn to her lips, and I couldn't pay attention to what she was saying. All I could think about was how much I wanted to kiss her. If I did, would she be shocked?

Suddenly she stopped talking. She was looking at me expectantly. I searched my mind for what she just said. "What about you? What do you dream of doing? What would you like to accomplish with your life?"

I hadn't been asked that question in a very long time.

"I don't know. When I was younger I wanted to be a pilot, or an astronaut." I chuckled, thinking how juvenile that sounded. I should have a new dream by now. I shrugged. "Maybe I would be a driver?"

"Like race cars?"

I nodded. "Yeah, maybe."

She prodded me with questions, and I plied her with more of my own. It was dark when Alexandra looked at her watch and gasped. Standing abruptly, she said, "We've been here for two hours! I need to get home."

Grudgingly, I stood with her, and we turned toward her sister's place. I had that feeling you get when you walk home at the end of a school year, or when you finish a favorite movie: a sweet sadness mingled with deep joy.

The way Alexandra looked at me as she listened and the way she rested her hand on my forearm as I told her stories from Spofford made me feel like she was the only girl in the world who would be able to understand my past. Alexandra was beautiful inside and out. Intelligent and sweet. I didn't know any other girl like her. I may have been only sixteen, but I already knew I wanted to marry her someday.

We were just outside the big Catholic church across the street from her sister's house when I felt panic grab hold of my gut. My evening with Alexandra was almost over, and I hadn't confessed my feelings.

I stopped in my tracks. Alexandra stopped too.

I wiped a hand across the back of my neck. It had to be now. If I didn't say something now, I would burst, but I was suddenly scared of her response. "Alexandra?"

"Yes?"

My hands were shaking. I had never been this nervous with a girl before. Probably because I had never cared this much before. "I think you know I like you. I really like you."

She nodded, but her expression was hard to read. Her hands gripped the handles of the stroller, which blocked me from being close to her.

I walked around it to stand beside her. I slid my hand underneath her wrist and pulled her hand into my own. "I want you to be my girlfriend."

She looked at me a moment, then glanced down at her sleeping niece. She lifted her gaze to meet mine and nodded.

Butterflies flooded my stomach. *That was a yes!*

I turned her toward me and kissed her soundly. I wanted to cry with happiness. I wanted to laugh. I could barely stand still. "I'll come see you tomorrow at work."

She nodded again.

The warm glow of streetlamps lit the orange leaves of the tree behind us, and I was suddenly struck by the beauty of this once-ordinary street. The church looked palatial. And Alexandra—stunning, angelic Alexandra—was my girlfriend.

9

A Real Bad Apple

"Want to come over to my place tomorrow after school? My mom wants to meet you," I asked as I walked Alexandra home one night. When I told my parents I had a girlfriend, they weren't exactly pleased, but I thought if they could just meet Alexandra, they wouldn't worry so much.

"Meet your mom?" Alexandra's tone made it sound like a big deal.

I took her hand in mine. "They're going to love you. You're Dominican, so that's already a million points in your favor."

Alexandra chuckled.

"So you'll come?"

"Yes, I'll come."

I was right. Within minutes of meeting Alexandra, Mami pulled me aside. "I like this one. And not just because she's Dominican. . . . As long as you keep up with your studies," Mami whispered to me in Spanish, "then you can date her."

I think I would have kept seeing Alexandra with or without Mami's blessing, but I was glad to have it.

Alexandra's family was a different story. Her sister-in-law Cecilia knew our family. Cecilia's brother had married my aunt and knew about my stint in juvie, which meant Alexandra's sister knew all about it too. I could just imagine the conversation. "Oh yes, Herman was in a gang. He was arrested for stealing. He spent time in juvenile. That's why they sent him to live with his grandparents, and then he caused them so much trouble they had to send him back. A real bad apple," Cecilia would say in hushed, conspiratorial tones.

Alexandra would try to defend me. "That's all in the past. He's totally changed. Do you think I would go out with a gangster?"

Her sister would get angry and call her naïve. Her brother-in-law would lecture her and quote my sins.

I would have to be extra careful around them.

The problem with reinventing oneself is that, at times, your old self will rear its ugly head.

Alexandra and I were walking past a mall one day when some punk kid decided to run his mouth off at us. Without thinking, I pulled a knife from my pocket and pointed it at his chest.

He pulled back, fear in his eyes, but his reaction was nothing compared to Alexandra's. Her gasp was followed by a scream. "What are you doing? Don't do it!"

An older guy who was walking past us felt the need to chime in. "Hey man, don't do it. It's not worth it." He looked like he had some experience.

It shook me. I almost dropped my knife.

The mouthy kid turned and ran.

Alexandra grabbed my arm with tears in her eyes. "Why would you do something like that?"

I was ashamed. "Sorry, baby. I'm sorry. I don't know what I was thinking."

"Why do you even have a knife? What are you doing with that thing?" A tear traced a path down her cheek, and a knot grew in my stomach.

"Alexandra, baby . . . I'm sorry. You know that's not me. I'm not like that anymore."

She pulled back. "Then what was that?" The shock and fear in her voice were replaced with steel. "I can't be pulled into—"

"You won't!" My voice sounded more plaintive than I'd even expected it to. "I'm not going to carry a knife anymore. I swear."

Her eyes narrowed, assessing me.

I pulled her into a hug. "Did I scare you, baby? I'm sorry."

She rested her head against my chest for a second before answering. "I'm not afraid you'll do something to me, Herman. . . . But I am afraid you will do something that will get you killed. Or arrested. I couldn't handle that."

I kissed the top of her head. "That won't happen. I promise."

10

CAN'T SMILE WITHOUT YOU

It was Thanksgiving. Icy winds blasted down our streets, carrying with them rotting leaves, plastic bags, and empty beer cans. I sat on the couch looking out the window at people passing by, arms raised and heads turned to shield their eyes against debris.

The weather was fitting. I felt cold inside and out. Alexandra had gone off with her family for the holiday. I didn't know what to do with myself when she wasn't with me. I had begged her to stay, but her family wouldn't allow it. She would be back the day after tomorrow, but it felt like a lifetime.

Papi was home for a couple of days, and Mami had cooked up a feast. My whole family was at the dinner table. But no matter how good the food was or how much I ate, I felt empty. I wanted to think up ways of punishing Alexandra for leaving, but I knew I couldn't follow through with them.

"Alexandra, do you know how miserable I was? I couldn't even eat," I said when she finally got back.

She smiled and kissed my cheek.

I pulled away. "I'm being serious. You didn't even call. Your family doesn't believe in phones?" My voice was rising. The more I looked at her with her soft smile and impossibly magnetic eyes, the angrier I became.

It seemed like she didn't even care that we had been separated all that time. But the angrier I got, the softer she looked. I didn't want her sympathy. I turned to leave.

Alexandra grabbed my arm and tugged me back. "Herman, baby, I missed you too."

She rested her head against my back and wrapped her arms around my stomach. I could feel a spot of warmth on my shoulder where she kissed me.

My heart fluttered. It was rare for her to kiss me first. I turned in her arms and she lifted her head; our kiss made up for the time we'd been apart.

Prom night with Alexandra

Something changed from that point. By Christmas, I knew she was just as in love with me as I was with her. She was my world and I was hers. Neither of us cared two cents what anyone thought of us together. Her family would just have to deal with the fact that we were in love.

In my room that summer, Alexandra helped me pack for our trip to the Dominican Republic. We had planned to go to celebrate the end of school, but I also wanted to propose to her there. It would be so romantic.

"Herman, what is this?" Alexandra held up my little black book.

"You don't know what it is?" I chuckled.

I opened it for her, flipping through the well-worn pages. Before Alexandra, I had been a bit of a ladies' man; my black book was fuller than most.

"Why would you even keep that?" Alexandra's tone was acid. "Get rid of it."

"Aww, baby, you jealous?" I teased.

Her eyes narrowed, and I felt a cold energy roll off her.

"Get rid of it," she commanded again.

I felt my ire rise. It's not like I was the only one who had dated.

"What about all the guys you flirt with—"

She shot up from my bed and stood with her hands on her hips, her face inches from my own. "Are you kidding me right now? You know I cut myself off from all my guy friends. I don't even talk to my girlfriends anymore. We are always together. It's just me and you."

"Fine. If it makes you happy, I'll get rid of it!" My anger helped cover my guilty conscience.

By the time we left for the airport, peace had been restored. We linked arms and together pushed our luggage cart toward the check-in desk. We giggled and kissed for the entire length of the line.

———

Casa de Campo Resort was situated on one of the most beautiful beaches in the Caribbean. We dropped our bags off at our villa, headed for the beach, and spent the afternoon frolicking in the warm turquoise waters and relaxing in each other's arms on the white-sand beach.

It would have been perfect, but niggling in the back of our minds was fear for the future: Where we would live? How we would pay the rent?

I wanted to propose at sunset. I thought it would be easy. We had talked about it so much, and I had no doubt she would say yes, but my hand still shook as I held hers and gave voice to the words I had been practicing in my head.

"Will you marry me, Alexandra?" I was surprised that my voice sounded strong and determined when my insides felt like Jell-O.

There was a glimmer of tears in her eyes as she nodded her head—happy tears, I hoped. "Yes, I will marry you."

I exhaled.

The future was one big question mark, but at least we would face it together.

———

We left the next morning to visit our families. The long drive from La Romana to Bonao gave me hours to panic about meeting with her parents. Alexandra tried to distract me with funny stories about them, but it just reinforced for me how different our families were from each other.

Alexandra's parents didn't know we were in the country; we had wanted to surprise them. Now that seemed like a very bad idea. I convinced her we should stop in and see my family first, since we would be spending the most time with hers.

"I'd like you to meet my fiancée, Alexandra," I told my grandparents and the others who had gathered to welcome us. She was kissed and hugged by everyone—aunts, uncles, cousins, each one teasing us and welcoming her to the family.

When we got to her parents' place, I was sweating.

"¡Hola!" Alexandra called from the door.

There were screams of excitement and shouts of disbelief. They descended on Alexandra with kisses and hugs, completely ignoring me as I stood awkwardly by the door. It was several long minutes before they pulled away and greeted me politely.

"When did you get here?" her mother asked when we finally sat down together on their veranda with cool glasses of fresh juice in our hands. "How long can you stay?"

"We're staying at Casa de Campo, and we'll be—" Alexandra stopped midsentence. Her mother's bright smile had morphed into a dark frown.

Alexandra grabbed my arm. "We wanted to come and tell you . . . we're getting married."

Silence.

Alexandra tried to remain bright and positive. "Herman asked me to marry him . . . Mami . . . we're getting married."

Her mother's tone and expression were black. "You two had better be married when I come visit." Which, loosely translated, meant she wasn't happy about Alexandra's choice but she would rather we marry than "live in sin."

"Well, Alexandra," I said later, "we'd better get married or we will have your mother to deal with."

I held her hand tightly, and we shared a smile. We were going to be okay.

11

A HOME OF OUR OWN

I rattled a set of keys in front of Alexandra's face. "I did it. I got the job."

She squealed and gave me a kiss. "That's my baby. I knew you would."

I wouldn't say it was my dream job exactly, but working as a private driver for Photocircuits gave me experience and a paycheck, and it was a lot better than flipping burgers or bagging groceries.

"When do you start?" she asked.

I groaned. "I need to be up by five. I have to drive their employees to work."

I wasn't a big fan of early mornings. I was more likely to see a sunrise by staying up late than by waking up to catch it.

Alexandra grinned. "Now you know how I feel."

"Whatever. At least you can sleep on your morning commute," I teased.

Neither of us was really complaining. Alexandra had found a great job as an office clerk for an upscale department store in Manhattan.

"Don't forget we have to sign the papers tomorrow," she reminded me as we sprawled on the floor beside her bed. We'd found a cheap little basement apartment in College Point, Queens. Once we signed on the dotted line, it would be ours.

We had no furniture to move in. Nothing to hang on the walls. Apart from our clothes and a few necessities, we didn't have much to move. It was done in an afternoon.

Our first night in our new home would have looked rather pathetic to an outsider. We put our mattress on the bare floor and cuddled into each other's arms.

"Welcome home, Alexandra," I whispered in the darkness.

She tilted her face up to mine and kissed me.

It was shockingly quiet. Her sister's house and my parents' house were always so full of people. Here, it was just us. The creaking in the ceiling from the tenants walking overhead and the sound of sirens on the streets outside were nothing compared to the family tensions we had grown used to. This was bliss.

We had been living on our own for over a year when Alexandra and I started talking about having kids. Sure, we were young, but didn't that mean we would have more energy to take care of them?

"Don't you think we should get married first?" Alexandra asked. "Mami and Papi would be furious if I had a baby before we even got married."

"Okay, let's do it. Why wait?"

Alexandra was quiet for a minute, but when she answered her dark eyes were sparkling. "Okay. Let's!"

The Queens city clerk's office might not sound like the most romantic of locations, but with its gray columns and old-world charm, it seemed elegant enough for the occasion.

To say it was a small wedding might be an understatement. Alexandra and I stood in front of the justice of the peace with only my papi as a witness. We had discussed inviting all sorts of people, but having anyone else there would have caused a lot of drama, which would have taken away from the excitement of our day.

Alexandra was stunning. She didn't need a gown with puffed sleeves or a veil that trailed behind her for miles. She was the most beautiful bride I had ever seen.

"Do you, Herman Mendoza, take Alexandra Peña to be your lawfully wedded wife to have and to hold from this day forward?"

I felt a quiver run through me. It was a familiar line, but it was strange to actually say the words "I do" and know that this day—this moment—was one I would remember for the rest of my life.

The justice of the peace turned to Alexandra. "And do you, Alexandra Peña, take Herman Mendoza to be your lawfully wedded husband to have and to hold from this day forward?"

"I do." Her voice was strong and clear, music to my ears.

The ceremony couldn't have lasted much longer than five minutes. Alexandra and I signed the register, and Papi witnessed it. Before the ink was dry, we were ushered out and the next eager couple was led in.

I kissed Alexandra on the steps of the building. This wasn't a new beginning exactly. We had already been living together, but there was something different—a security in knowing that we were legally tied to one another. We weren't just a couple of kids playing house; we were recognized by the state as husband and wife. No one could come between us.

12

Baby, Oh Baby

"Baby, I'm pregnant!"

It's amazing how combinations of three words can hold so much power. *I love you. I'll marry you. Baby, I'm pregnant.*

It was an early June morning in 1990 when Alexandra shook me awake.

My body seemed to understand the words before my mind could register them. My heart raced and my hands shook as I rubbed the sleep from my eyes. "What?"

Alexandra giggled and kissed my cheek. "You're going to be a daddy."

"What?" I asked again. I didn't believe my ears. "You're . . . baby, you're . . . ?" I couldn't even say the word.

She nodded again.

"I'm going to be a dad? We're going to have a baby?"

"Yes. We are."

I was going to be a father! A laugh erupted from deep inside. I couldn't contain my joy. My whole body shook. I jumped up and flopped down again on the side of the bed, pulling her into a hug and kissing her all over her face.

It took approximately three minutes for a huge sense of responsibility to hit me. It wasn't heavy, nor did it cause any sort of remorse. It was like I had awakened to my purpose. In less than a year there would be a little mouth to feed. Babies needed all sorts of stuff just to keep them alive, didn't they?

"You worried, baby?" Alexandra must have seen the gears spinning in my brain.

I turned over and rested my head in her lap. She stroked my forehead. "Aren't you excited?"

"Of course I am," I assured her, drawing her toward me so I could kiss her head.

She moved to stand and pulled me up. "Let's tell your mom. She's going to be so excited!"

She was right. Mami had always wanted a daughter, and now that some of her boys were married, her hope for a girl in the family was renewed. My brother Emilio and his wife had announced that they were expecting a few months ago, and our news was going to double Mami's chances for a granddaughter.

We knocked on the door of my parents' house with a little more enthusiasm than usual. We tried to play it cool, but there was no hiding the silly grins on our faces.

"¿Qué está pasando? ¿Por qué esas sonrisas? Why are you smiling like that?" she asked as she opened the door and let us in.

"¡Vamos a tener un bebé, Mami! We're going to have a baby!"

Mami let out a little whoop of excitement. Everyone came running to hear the news. For the rest of the visit, Mami kept looking at Alexandra and smiling, her grin growing bigger and bigger.

There were all the questions you might expect.

"We don't want to find out the gender," we said. "We will be happy either way."

"It will be a girl," Mami assured us. Of course, she had said the same to Emilio and his wife.

Alexandra nodded. "Yes, I'm hoping for a girl too."

I didn't know what I would prefer. A boy would be great—I could teach him basketball. We could go to baseball games together. But a girl would be so cute—a little princess to spoil. Alexandra and I agreed we just wanted a happy, healthy baby.

For that, I would need to tighten my belt and find another job. As much as I liked driving, I wasn't confident I could support our family on that salary, and Alexandra wouldn't be able to work for a while once she'd had the baby. I knew my brothers Emilio and Dante were bringing in good money running drugs. They even invited me to join them. I had promised Alexandra and Mami that I wouldn't do stuff like that anymore, but going into business with my brothers was tempting.

Emilio and his wife had their baby, an adorable little boy, in July. We all loved him, but this put even more pressure on Alexandra and me to produce a girl. Maybe we should have found out the gender. Then we wouldn't have felt pressure as we waited.

Fortunately, we were given an escape in those final weeks of Alexandra's pregnancy. Her brother and his wife were also expecting. "Why don't you come on up to Rhode Island? There is a great hospital here, and you can stay with us until you have the baby," they said. Being guests for three weeks wasn't the most comfortable of situations, but with another mouth to feed, we would be hurting for money.

"You can't make that drive every day. It's too much," Alexandra argued.

"I can come on the weekends. They'll be able to take better care of you than I can."

Her eyes were teary, and though I didn't like the idea of being separated, it just made sense.

Alexandra's face scrunched up.

"Are you all right?" I had been watching her carefully for days, waiting for any sign that she was in labor. Alexandra rubbed her stomach. It was tight and swollen, and she looked so uncomfortable.

She let out a breath. "Yeah. I'm all right. . . . I'm just so far past my due date."

I sat up straighter, my eyes trained on her stomach. I'm not sure what I expected to see.

After a little while, she gasped again and rubbed her stomach. "They scheduled an appointment to induce on February 19."

———

I could feel my blood pressure start to rise. This was it. "Should I get your bag?"

Alexandra laughed. "I'm having some small contractions, but they're still too far apart." She acted like she had done this a million times before, but I could see a nervousness in her eyes and a slight tremble in her lips.

She waited through a couple more contractions before she agreed to go to the hospital. I already had her bags in the car. I took her by the arm and led her outside, scrambling to get just ahead of her and open her door.

The pains continued to come. Once at the hospital, we spent the rest of the day waiting to meet our child.

By 2:00 P.M. the next day, things began to progress quickly. The contractions were five minutes apart. Then three. And then they got stronger. Alexandra looked like she was in real pain.

I couldn't bear to see her in such agony. I dashed into the hall to catch my breath. I started to pace. I was just twenty-one, and I was going to be a dad. What were we thinking? I needed some liquid courage. Fortunately, I had thought to bring a bottle of Johnnie Walker to calm my nerves. I took a couple of swigs. The heat moving down my throat provided a temporary distraction.

"Mr. Mendoza?" a dour-looking nurse called from Alexandra's room.

I jogged to the door. "Yes—that's me."

"You can come in now. It's time."

They placed a blood pressure cuff around her arm and attached a pulse monitor to her finger. Another nurse checked her temperature while Alexandra groaned in pain.

Suddenly, I wasn't just nervous, I was afraid. What if something happened to Alexandra?

By the time her mother arrived, Alexandra and I were both

terrified. Tears were streaming down Alexandra's face. How much more could she take? Another contraction was building, and her mother and I each took one of her hands.

"Get away from me! You have no idea how I feel," she screamed. "I'm in pain!"

I was sure it was an understatement.

A nurse came in to check how dilated she was, only to rush back out of the room. She came back in minutes later with the doctor. Suddenly, everything began to happen at once. I was handed a hat and gown, and Alexandra was draped in a green sheet. They were placing her feet in stirrups and telling her to push. My mother-in-law stayed by Alexandra's side to hold her hand, and I grabbed my camera.

"What are you taking pictures for? Nobody wants to see that," the head nurse chastised.

"I do!" Alexandra suddenly yelled. "Don't tell my husband he can't. It's our baby."

Her words turned into a grunt as she pushed. And then there was our daughter, attached by a long umbilical cord to her mother. I barely had time to snap a few pictures before the doctor placed the squirming, slippery infant in my arms.

She was so small. Her arms and legs explored the space around her as I held her close. Her tiny cries were the most beautiful thing I had ever heard.

It was so surreal. Alexandra and I had a daughter. This little baby was coming home with us. I wrapped her little fingers around my own, studying the paper-thin nails, amazed at the strength of her grip.

She would grow up with Alexandra and me as her parents. For better or for worse, her perception of fatherhood would be defined by me.

"You should call your mother." Alexandra's voice was calm and gentle.

Now that the intense pain had passed, she radiated peace.

"You are amazing. You know that, right?"

Alexandra grinned.

I picked up the receiver from the beige phone beside her bed and dialed my parents' number. It barely had a chance to ring when I heard Mami's "¿Hola?" on the other end of the line.

I leaned close to Alexandra so she could hear too. "¡Es una niña, Mami!"

It's a girl. Three more life-changing words.

13

A SLIPPERY SLOPE

"Herman! It's your turn," Alexandra called from our bedroom. It was the third time Samantha had woken up that evening. I had promised to be a supportive husband. I wanted to make sure that Alexandra had an easy, peaceful recovery.

"Where are the wipes?" I asked as I entered. It was impossible to remember where Alexandra kept everything.

"Right there, on the dresser."

"And the diapers?"

Alexandra sighed heavily and began to get up. I waved her away.

"I'll get it, just tell me."

She pointed to the dresser. I searched again. They were right behind the wipes. I felt like an idiot.

"What did you eat?" I teased as I took Sam from her mother's arms. "She's smiling at me!"

"It's probably just gas." Alexandra laughed, but as I glanced at her, I saw an uncommon look on her face. She was proud of me.

I looked around our drab bedroom. How could she be proud of me when I wasn't proud of myself? There were three of us now, and our dog, Sammy. I needed to find us a new place.

"You have to watch her," Alexandra instructed as she tucked her shirt into her slacks. "You wouldn't believe the things I fished out of her mouth yesterday."

I groaned. It was usually Mami who watched Sam while Alexandra and I worked. But I had the day off, so it was up to me to hold down the fort.

Sam was learning to walk. If I turned away for a minute, she would be in another room, investigating something potentially life threatening.

By the time Alexandra got home that night, Sam and I were asleep on the couch. Alexandra gently plucked Sam from my arms, causing me to wake in a full panic. "I thought I dropped her!" I shouted.

When Samantha was just two years old, I was handed the pink slip. Bills were piling up, our credit cards were maxed out, and Alexandra and I were exhausted. I found a few jobs here and there—a parking attendant, a driver for a rental car company. They were easy jobs with decent pay, but they never lasted long.

I felt like I was failing my family. Life felt overwhelming. How could I climb out of this death spiral?

Once Alexandra and Sam were in bed, I left for the nearest bar. I just needed to ease some of the stress that had been building.

It was sometime after my second or third beer that I decided on a change. Dante and Emilio ran their own business and were bringing in piles of cash. Yes, what they were doing was illegal, but at least they could take care of their families. They had nice clothes and impressive homes while I was working my butt off like a chump.

Like my parents, I was basically a slave to whoever decided to hand me a paycheck. It was time to talk to my brothers and see how I could do what they were doing. Not dealing necessarily—I had made that vow as a teenager to live clean, and I meant to keep it—but I was sure there had to be something I could do.

"What's up?" Dante asked as he sat beside me at the bar the next night.

"Nothin'," I lied.

He ordered a drink and got me another Johnnie Walker.

"How's Alexandra and Sam?"

"Good. You should come by sometime."

He nodded but didn't say anything more, obviously waiting for an explanation for the sudden invitation to meet.

"How's business?" I asked.

"Good."

Another silence stretched between us.

He looked me over and smiled. "You want in, don't you?"

I shrugged. To be honest, I still wasn't sure. Emilio and Dante had been selling since we were young and had made it into a real business. It wasn't like the dinky drug deals I had done as a kid. They even had an office.

"I don't want to do nothing illegal," I finally blurted.

Dante leaned in close, his voice low. "Tell you what. We need a guy to count cash. You won't be selling. We can give you a few thousand bucks if you help us out."

That didn't sound bad. I wasn't saying I would do it, but I was interested.

"Why don't you try it out. Meet me on Friday, and you can give it a shot." He sounded nonchalant.

Yeah, why not? Counting money was not drug dealing. That wasn't so different from what Alexandra did at Citibank . . . and I trusted my brothers. They seemed to have all sorts of protections in place. I nodded slowly. Working with them would be an easy way to make a lot of cash and still not deal directly with drugs. It was a win-win. "Okay. I'll do it."

"Yeah? You're in?"

"I'm in."

He held up his glass and clinked it against mine before finishing it in a single shot.

14

COCAINE AND CRIME

I drove through Forest Hills looking for the address Dante gave me. I passed kosher delis and goldsmiths, fine dining restaurants and luxury condominiums. This was obviously a wealthier part of town.

The office building was several stories high and ten streets over from the Long Island Expressway, safely tucked away from main thoroughfares. I parked around the corner and made my way to the front entrance. The list of names beside the buzzer was an impressive who's who of doctors and lawyers. I wondered if any of them knew that the base of my brothers' operations was hidden in plain sight.

The night before I had purchased a beeper. I toyed with the gray plastic device in my hand. I had always envied the yuppie business-men, doctors, and celebrities who walked around with beepers, making urgent calls in response to the short numeric codes that appeared on the screen. Beepers were a marvel of technology. Now I carried with me that little marker of success. I liked it. It was real Hollywood movie kind of stuff.

My brothers' organization had fairly simple codes. There was no real reason to get too cloak-and-dagger.

"If you have any problems," Dante had said, "message 505 to me or Emilio."

I wrote it down in my little notebook. "Why 505?"

Dante tapped the notebook where I had just scribbled the number.

"What does that look like?"

"Ahh . . . SOS."

He nodded.

"And when you get to the main entrance of the building, message me 77. Don't talk to anyone. Don't try and ring the buzzer. Just beep me. . . . You got that?"

I nodded.

Now, as I stood outside the entrance and messaged his beeper, my heart pounded. I was really doing this. Stealth and secrecy were now part of my world.

It was a few seconds before there was a buzzing sound and a click as the lock on the door released.

The first thing I noticed as I entered the office was all the cash on the floor. There were tens, twenties, and fives scattered everywhere and dozens of piles of fifties and hundreds. An electric energy ran through me at the thought of being a part of this lifestyle, but somehow I wasn't afraid.

On top of a dresser by the counting machines lay two MAC-10 machine guns. I wandered over to them for a closer look. I'd never seen anything so cool in my entire life. I wondered if they'd ever had to use them.

"Herman, come here." Dante had to shout for me to hear him. In a corner of one of the rooms, a television was turned up full blast to cover the sound of the counting machines.

I walked over to the desk he was sitting at, which was piled high with bills.

"Watch me."

He took a handful and sorted them by denomination, then rotated them so they all faced the same direction. He was very particular.

I was impatient to get going, curious how much money could be in this room. I started off strong, sorting and flipping and stacking and counting. But by midday, I started slowing down. My shoulders ached from leaning over the desk, and I felt I could use a stiff drink.

As fascinating as it all was, there was so much money that the job was almost monotonous. By the end of the day, I had counted $1.2 million.

We kept 15 percent. I counted out $180,000. Emilio and Dante were really onto something. Easy cash and a quick turnaround? *¡Claro que sí!*

We loaded the rest into industrial-size laundry bags. I didn't know what kind of office could produce so many large bags of dirty laundry, but it seemed to be a good enough cover. I lifted two onto each shoulder and headed downstairs after the other guys.

Two guys from the Colombian cartel waited in the lobby. We handed over the bags and watched as they crossed the street and tossed them in the back of a dark commercial van.

Apart from the guns, and the stacks of illicit cash, it all felt very much like any other office job. I was practically a white-collar worker.

15

Rollin' in It

"Nine thousand five . . . and ten," Dante counted out my pay.

After working six days, I was walking out with just over $10,000. It was a beautiful, natural high.

I went home that night with gifts for Alexandra and Sam. I had taken the job for them, after all. I should spoil them a little—but not too much or Alexandra might get angry. She knew I had taken a job with Emilio and Dante but didn't know the details. I was pretty sure she didn't want to.

When Alexandra went to put Sam to bed, I pulled out a bottle of Johnnie Walker Blue. It had been a long time since I had splurged on a whole bottle of Johnnie, but never in my life had I bought Blue Label. Its $180 price tag gave me only a moment's hesitation. I'd spent almost $1,000 on my way home, but I still had $9,000, and I would get paid again at the end of next week.

I poured myself a couple of fingers of the smooth signature scotch drink and tossed it back, relishing the feeling of liquid warmth traveling down my throat. This was the good life.

When I arrived at work the next morning, the news channel was blaring. The guys and I laughed as we listened to the anchor recite the latest statistics on the city's "war on drugs." With the increase in dealer arrests, demand went up, meaning that our guys could charge more. We were the link between the cartels and the people.

"You coming out? I have some guys for you to meet." Emilio stood with Dante by the door. He raised his eyebrows. "Time to party."

Dante gave a lazy smile. He wasn't quite as much the party animal as Emilio, but he still liked to have a good time.

A few minutes later, we pulled up to the Copacabana. Live music filtered out into the street. It was a world away from the bland white space of the office. The Copacabana throbbed with the rhythm of bongo drums, and rainbow splinters of light reflected off multiple disco balls.

We worked our way through writhing, jumping crowds. Everywhere I looked there were recognizable faces, a veritable who's who of celebrities. But we weren't there to rub shoulders with the rich and famous.

"This way!" Emilio waved me over.

He stood beside a man with leathery skin and dark eyes. The man's collar was popped, and the sleeves of his expensive sport coat were rolled up to the elbow, revealing muscled forearms. He held out his hand and I shook it. No one had to tell me this guy was part of the Colombian cartel, but Dante made the introductions anyway.

The music made it hard to hear, but I surmised this man was one of the big guys and on really friendly terms with my brothers. He led us toward a reserved VIP table where we were greeted by several women clothed in designer cocktail dresses showing off tanned legs and toned arms. They rearranged themselves until they sat sandwiched between us.

Not even a month ago, I was struggling to put food on the table, and now I was sitting at a VIP table in the most popular club in New York drinking champagne and scotch.

The skinny redhead beside me rested a hand on my leg and leaned close. "Herman, was it? What do you do?"

There was a slight tightening in the muscles of my shoulders and a hiccup in my pulse before the lie tripped off my tongue. "I own a business . . . contracting."

"You're a builder?"

I nodded an affirmation.

Her eyes lit up, and she tossed her mass of ginger hair over her shoulder. "I admire men who work with their hands."

She was flirting with me, and I didn't quite know how to respond.

I glanced at my brothers. Emilio was deep in conversation with the cartel rep, but Dante was flirting with two other girls. It was strange to see them in this setting—they acted differently at home. The scene reminded me of *Scarface*; I liked that movie, but it also served as a warning. Some lines shouldn't be crossed.

I turned to the redhead. She was tipping back a glass of champagne. I let her finish before I asked, "What do you do for work?"

She laughed. The light tinkling sound seemed rehearsed. "Can you guess?"

I looked her over. Everything about this girl looked measured and manicured. She was skin and bones, but her gold lamé cocktail dress made her look like she had stepped from the pages of *Vogue*. Heavy makeup accentuated her high cheekbones and full lips. She had money coming in from somewhere, but I doubted it was from her day job.

"Stewardess?"

With a laugh, she poured me a drink. "Men and their fantasies."

The champagne was good. The bubbles pricked at my tongue, and it warmed my throat with its spicy sweetness. I could play the game for a little while, I figured. It might be fun.

The sun was starting to come up as I attempted to put my key into the lock of our new apartment door. My eyes refused to focus, and my hands wouldn't obey me. I held the key tightly in both hands and closed one eye to see more clearly. There was a rattle and a thunk as the dead bolt turned and the door swung open.

Alexandra stood in her nightgown, hands on her hips and tears in her eyes. "You're ruining our lives!" she cried.

She had warned me the night before not to come home drunk.
I guess she meant it. I stood up straight and attempted a look of
nonchalance. A difficult look to affect when your vision is blurred.

She said nothing more—just stood near the door, watching my
halting progress as I stumbled my way toward the couch. "I'm
sorry, baby."

"Go to bed, Herman."

My head felt heavy as I nodded.

I wasn't going to tell her I'd already been to bed that night. She
might have suspected my occasional infidelity, but if she ever asked,
I would deny it. My brothers and my entourage would support me
in my deception. If Alexandra questioned them about my whereabouts, they would always have my back. I told myself there was
no reason to hurt her with the truth.

I had been in business with my brothers for almost a year, and
I wasn't just counting money anymore. I was hosting parties and
making deals. I was a real partner. The only downside was that
when there was a drought, like when a shipment failed to get across
the border, we grew short on product and clients went elsewhere.
This was one of those dry weeks.

We'd spent hours hoping and waiting for our shipment to get
through, but in the end, one of the cartel guys ended up in jail and
it had been confiscated.

Alexandra couldn't blame me for needing a little release. She
was enjoying all the perks of the business. New car, new clothes,
new waterside condo. But still she nagged me. The day before, she
had held up a Bible and shouted, "We're better off eating a crust
of bread than a steak that was gotten illegally!"

Like she was so Christian.

I lay back on our bed and closed my eyes on the spinning room.

16

THE POCONOS

I almost missed the chirp of my beeper. I was entertaining some clients at one of my favorite restaurants, and the chatter around the table grew louder with each round of drinks.

I glanced down at it. 505. I almost spat out my drink. I put down my scotch and excused myself. "What's up?" I asked as soon as Dante answered the phone.

"They have Jay."

Jay had been with us for a while—longer than I had been in the business. He knew names and faces. He knew contacts and pickup points. If the police had him and he ratted us out, we'd be in deep trouble.

"When?"

"About an hour ago."

I felt a tingle run up my spine. An hour was a long time. There could be guys looking for us already. I spun around, looking for any sign that I was being watched, but everyone looked suspicious to me now.

I hung up and hotfooted it to my car. I had to get home.

"Alexandra!" I called as I pushed through the door.

She sauntered out of our bedroom carrying Sam.

"Alexandra, baby. It's time to move."

She cocked her head, assessing how drunk I was. I wasn't completely sober—I rarely was—but I wasn't drunk.

"Why would we move again? We've barely unpacked from our last move."

I shook my head. *Why can't she just do what I say instead of questioning everything?* "I just think it would be better to live outside the city. Somewhere safer for Sam."

Alexandra glanced down at our sleeping toddler.

"But we're happy here. And this neighborhood is pretty safe."

"Baby, if I tell you it's not safe, can't you just believe me?"

She looked unconvinced.

"Listen, they picked up one of our guys. I don't want no one sniffing around here, bothering you."

Her face registered the shock I had been feeling.

"We could try the Poconos. You love it there. Think how much safer it would be."

The Poconos was one of our favorite vacation spots. It was so quiet and beautiful.

Alexandra nodded. "We could get a house of our own."

"Yes! Absolutely."

"Somewhere surrounded by trees." She was coming around.

"Of course!"

For a minute Alexandra seemed lost in thought. Her mind was already traveling the roads and byways of Pennsylvania. "Okay," she finally said. "Okay, let's do it."

I took her face in my hands and kissed her. "It's gonna be great. You'll see."

It didn't take long to find the perfect place. A small house in a gated community. We moved out of our condo at record speed.

After the movers left, Sam fell asleep on a blanket on the floor of our new living room, and I felt like it was safe for me to go.

I found Alexandra staring out the back windows at the woods behind the house. She was hugging herself tightly and running her hands up and down her arms. "Creepy, isn't it?" She nodded toward the tree line.

I couldn't help laughing. "Trust me, New York is far more dangerous than those woods."

I pulled her back against my chest and hugged her tight. I felt her shiver. "Aww, baby. Don't be scared. Nothing is going to get you here."

I kissed the top of her head. "I need to go. I promised the guys I would be back tonight."

She spun around. "What?"

"I'm heading back. I have some—"

"But we just moved in!" Tears pooled in her eyes.

"Aww, baby. I'll be back on the weekend. I promise. Just get some rest. It was a long day and you're tired." I figured I had better leave quick before the crying started.

The truth was I had a date with Daria, a waitress at a restaurant I went to a few times a week. She was pretty, though much older, and there were plenty of other guys who wanted to be with her. I knew she liked me right away, and I was flattered. I had ended up at her apartment on more than one occasion. She knew that I was married but didn't seem to mind. If anything, she seemed to make an even bigger effort to spend time with me.

After a long day of moving, it would be nice to share a couple of drinks with her and let her spoil me. I pulled up outside Daria's restaurant and called her from my cell phone. She waved from the doorway, her phone to her ear. "Come in. I have dinner for you."

"Hello?" Alexandra's voice sounded tired.

"Alexandra, baby. How are you feeling today?"

There was an angry silence on the other end of the phone.

"Did you sleep okay? How is Sam?"

"Fine."

I didn't expect her to be excited to hear from me, but I hadn't realized she would be so angry. I probably needed to give her a little more time.

"Listen, Alexandra. I'll need to call you later, but I just wanted to see that you were all right. . . . I love you."

More silence.

"I'll call you later, okay?"

That final moment before we hung up I was sure I heard a small hiccup before the click of the receiver. I felt bad for Alexandra. I would bring her some flowers when I went home Saturday, something to remind her that Pennsylvania offered her and Sam a better life.

17

THE MISTRESS

I woke up at our place in Pennsylvania with a killer hangover. Alexandra was climbing back into bed, her face as pallid as my own. She wiped at the corners of her mouth.

"Are you okay?"

She smiled. "I will be in eight months or so."

What was that supposed to mean?

Her grin widened as my brain made sense of her cryptic response. I bolted upright. "You're pregnant?"

Alexandra nodded as I grabbed her into a tight hug. She laughed. "Are you excited?"

She wasn't showing at all, but I couldn't help rubbing and kissing her stomach. I was thrilled. We had wanted another child. Sam was walking, and she would be out of diapers soon.

"You'll go with me for the ultrasound, right?"

"Of course, baby. Why wouldn't I?"

Alexandra shrugged. "I just wanted to make sure you wouldn't have to be away on business."

I kissed her again. "I wouldn't miss it."

It was late when I got back to the apartment that I rented for Daria. She was sleeping on the sofa with the TV on when I walked in.

"Daria? Baby? I'm back."

Daria stretched her arms and her back before opening her eyes. "You're late today."

She reached her hand toward me, and I helped her up.

"I wanted to wait up for you, but I was just so tired." She wrapped her arms around my neck. "I have some pretty big news."

"Oh? What's that?"

She took a deep breath. The pause and the breath were just long enough to make me nervous.

"I'm pregnant."

"You're what?"

I didn't mean to shout, but I couldn't have been more shocked. I found my way to the dining table and sank down onto the closest chair.

Daria followed me and pulled a chair out across from mine. "Are you upset?"

I was. I pulled at my hair, angry at my predicament. How had this happened? If Alexandra found out, she'd kill me. It would destroy us. I couldn't lose Alexandra.

"Do you want me to . . . get rid of it?"

I couldn't speak. I absolutely didn't want any part in something like that. Abortion, in my mind, was murder. But the fact that I would have another child, outside of my marriage, was a scary scenario to contemplate.

"I want to keep it," she said when I failed to respond.

My head felt heavy as I nodded.

It was the right thing to do, but with those few words, it felt like she had tied a noose around my neck. For Daria to be pregnant at the same time as Alexandra seemed like a cruel joke. Daria was my good-time girl. Now I would have to support her and the baby for the rest of my life.

I pushed back from the table and turned to the door. "I need to get some air." What I really meant was that I was going to get drunk and forget all about this nightmare.

———

Alexandra lay back on the vinyl table of the ultrasound room. She rolled up the end of her hospital gown, exposing her tanned belly, which had just a hint of roundness.

"Would you like to know the gender?" the technician asked as she squeezed gel across Alexandra's stomach.

"We would," Alexandra and I said in unison.

The static on the black-and-white screen suddenly arranged itself into distinct shapes as the technician moved the ultrasound's wand across Alexandra's lower abdomen.

She pointed at the moving shapes. "There's the head and arms. Baby looks a good size."

She moved the wand again, shoving it harder against Alexandra's belly. Alexandra looked up at me and squeezed my hand.

"You can see the feet . . . and right there . . . you can see we've got ourselves a baby boy!"

"A boy?" Alexandra sounded as if she couldn't quite believe it, even though she'd told me she thought it was a boy.

I kissed Alexandra. "We have a son!"

I was already sure of the name for my son. Adam.

"I'm not going!"

"But, Daria, baby, it'll be so much better for you there. Cleaner air, better schools. Think of the baby."

She shook her head again. "I'm not doing it. My friends are here. You're here. Why would I move?"

"Fine. Have it your way!"

It was an argument Daria and I had had almost every day since Alexandra's ultrasound. Three weeks of coaxing and cajoling to get her to move somewhere Alexandra wouldn't discover her. But Daria wouldn't give.

I grabbed my wallet and keys.

"Where are you going?" Daria shouted.

"Out!"

I'd promised Dante I'd go to a party with him at the home of a music producer. I wanted Daria to worry that I was out with other girls. She needed to know she didn't own me.

18

NO WAY, NOT ME

I shook my head to clear it. The dotted yellow line in the center of I-80 on the way to Pennsylvania kept separating into two distinct lines. They waved back and forth, mesmerizing me.

Alexandra always complained about how much I drank, and since I would be with her for the weekend, I thought I would get a weekend's worth of drinking in before heading home.

I pressed down on the accelerator, looking down to watch the needle on my speedometer swing to the right. Then I dozed off.

Bang!

I was flung forward in my seat. My seat belt tightened against my rib cage, forcing the air from my lungs.

My car spun to a stop.

My head reeled, but I was more alert and sober than I had been seconds before. What had I hit? *Please, God. Don't let it be another vehicle.*

I shook my head, hoping to clear it. My car was facing the wrong way in the lane, and my headlights illuminated a crumpled guardrail.

I could have killed someone. I could be dead right now.

I heard the roar of an eighteen-wheeler approaching. The driver was honking his horn frantically. Panicked, I restarted my car, spun the wheel, and pressed hard on the accelerator. I had to get home. If I got stopped right now, I'd lose my license.

Alexandra must have heard me pull up, because she was waiting for me at the door when I walked in. I couldn't meet her eyes. I didn't want her to know what had happened. "Hey, baby, I'm tired. I'm just gonna hit the sack."

My words sounded jumbled, even to my ears. Her brow furrowed, and her eyes looked so incredibly sad. Defeated.

She helped me take off my shoes and pulled my arm across her shoulders. From this angle, I had a perfect view of her nicely rounded belly. "Hey, Adam. My boy!" I tried to speak, but I was sure the words were incomprehensible.

Alexandra led me to my side of the bed and sat me down. She took off my socks and put my legs up. "Sleep it off."

I closed my eyes and slept.

"Herman!" Alexandra shouted.

I winced. My head pounded, and my neck ached. I could feel every muscle in my body.

"What did you do?" She continued to shout as she came into our bedroom. "You were in an accident?"

I put a finger to my lips to shush her. That only made things worse.

"How could you do that? You could be dead right now, and our babies wouldn't have a father!" Tears streamed down her cheeks. "How can you be so selfish?"

I sat up and pulled her close. "Shh, baby, it's okay. I'm all right."

She pulled away from me. "It's not okay. Don't ever do something like that again. Just stay in New York if you're going to drink like that!"

"Never again. I promise."

When I drove home the following Friday night it was with a lightness that I hadn't experienced in a very long while. Alexandra was only weeks away from her due date and had been busy cleaning out the new nursery. Sam was three and had begun to take her role as a big sister seriously.

I drove through the gates to our neighborhood and pulled up to our beautiful home bathed in golden light from the streetlamps. I was a lucky man.

Alexandra opened the door before I reached it. She apparently was not feeling as happy and carefree as I was. Her face was grave, and her arms were crossed on top of her belly. I did a quick breath check—I didn't want her to have any reason to think I had been drinking. I'd had a couple of beers before I left, but I was not drunk.

"You have a girlfriend?"

I stopped in my tracks, mentally cursing whoever it was that blabbed.

"Baby, baby, there is no girlfriend. Who told you that? How could I cheat on you? It's absolutely not true."

I reached up to rub her arms, but she slapped my hands away.

"Oh really? So you're saying Carmen's lying to me, making up stories about pregnant girlfriends, for no reason?"

Carmen! Why would she do this? Didn't she know how upset Alexandra would be?

"Baby, she must have heard some weird rumor, but it's not true. I have you. I love you. Why would I have a girlfriend? That doesn't even make sense. I'd never cheat on you."

It was amazing how readily the lies tripped off my tongue. I almost believed them myself.

Alexandra cocked her head to the side, appraising me. She didn't look convinced, but she stood aside and let me come in. I spent the rest of the weekend acting the part of a doting husband and father.

When I got back to New York, I told Daria what had happened.

"So? Why should I care?" Her tone was surprisingly bland.

"I just want to make sure she doesn't find out. Maybe keep your head down for a bit. Don't go anywhere my family might see you."

She snorted. "Have you seen these ankles? I can't go anywhere for very long."

Her discomfort was my saving grace.

"They are pretty swollen. Why don't you come sit down." I flopped down on the sofa and patted the spot beside me.

———

Alexandra called me unexpectedly. I picked up, a little apprehensive. "Hello?"

"I'm at Daria's."

Three more life-changing words stopped me in my tracks. The steel in Alexandra's voice petrified me. My wife and my mistress, pregnant with my children, face-to-face. And I had no idea what they were saying to each other.

I learned later how Alexandra had checked the apartment address on the paper in her hands, then studied the woman who had answered the door. A relative of Alexandra's who often partied with me had met me at Daria's before. He told another family member, and the news spread.

"Are you Daria?"

The woman had nodded and barked, "What do you want?"

Alexandra cocked her head to the side. Carmen had said Daria was pregnant. This woman definitely wasn't. She leaned inside the door and saw another woman at the far end of the room, her back to the door. Alexandra's lips turned up in a cold grin. "I heard you're having an affair with my husband . . . but you don't look pregnant."

Alexandra's frosty tone was surprisingly effective at provoking a response. Something in Daria snapped. She turned and shuffled to the door, her pregnant belly on full display.

"I'm Daria." She ran a hand across her stomach. "Herman told me that you guys are not together." Daria took a threatening step forward. "You should just step back."

Alexandra's fists clenched and her face reddened, but she held it together. She dug the heavy cell phone out of her purse and dialed my number.

"Alexandra, baby—" I pleaded over the phone.

"She said you want a divorce."

"Honey, baby. You can't believe what she says. It was a onetime thing. The only reason there is still any connection is because she got pregnant. Baby, I promise you're the one I love. The only one."

That part was true. I didn't really love Daria. The world I had created for myself with Daria was, in my mind, a fantasy. Alexandra was the real thing. It was Alexandra I loved and wanted to protect.

Alexandra hung up and shoved the phone back in her purse. "He says you're lying."

Daria's face went pale. "I am not lying."

I met Alexandra back in Pennsylvania, intent on putting out the fires. Our conversation picked up where she had hung up.

"It really was a onetime thing."

"She looked pretty convinced that you were gonna leave me for her."

I shook my head, my heart and my eyes pleading for her to understand. "What do you want her to do? Do you want her to have an abortion?"

Alexandra's face morphed into an expression of horror. "No, of course not. It isn't that baby's fault." She rubbed her own belly as she said it. "Obviously she needs to have the baby."

"So what should I do?"

"You can stay with her. I won't interfere. You can still see your kids. I wish you the best."

I shook my head violently. "No. I told you it was just a onetime thing."

It wasn't. I knew, even as I said it, that on Monday evening I would be going back to Daria. But there was no way I'd ever admit that to Alexandra.

It was morning and I was drunk. *Still drunk* is more accurate. The sound of my phone ringing filtered through my inebriated fog.

"Herman?" It was Alexandra.

"Mmhmm?"

"I'm in labor. I'm already at the hospital."

I bolted upright. "I'm coming. I'm coming right now!"

I hung up and called for a driver. It was at least an hour and a half to the hospital, and I was in no condition to drive.

The driver pulled up to the hospital entrance, and I jumped out and ran through a labyrinth of long corridors to the maternity ward. When I found Alexandra, she was resting comfortably in a bed. Her contractions were not particularly strong with minutes in between.

"You're all right?"

She nodded and I patted her hand. "Good, good." I yawned. "Look, baby. I was up half the night. I am just going to run home and take a quick shower, okay? We still have lots of time, right?"

Not giving her a chance to answer, I trudged back down the hall and headed for the parking lot, where my driver still waited.

The shower felt good, and it washed away the stink of alcohol and cigarettes. I grabbed a change of clothes and styled my hair. We'd probably take pictures, and I wanted to look good.

I made sure the driver drove as quickly as possible on the way back to the hospital, and I retraced my route through the hallways to Alexandra's room.

I heard a baby's cry as I entered. The doctor was at the business end of Alexandra's bed, holding a wriggling infant. My son!

I had missed his birth by seconds.

I rushed forward, taking him from the doctor's hands. "Daddy's here."

He stopped crying.

I glanced up at Alexandra. "I think he recognizes my voice."

Alexandra met my joyful gaze with fury. I had failed her when she needed me, and now here I was just in time to steal the first touch from her.

My enthusiasm dimmed. I felt every inch the selfish dirtbag that I was.

I'm losing control of my life. It was a thought I had pushed from my mind many times, but seeing Alexandra looking at me with such condemnation, such sadness and disgust, I had to face it. I looked back down at my baby's face. I needed to do more. Be better.

———

"Herman, you're a father!" It was Daria's voice. "We have a girl."

My heart skipped a beat. "What did you say?"

"Come meet your daughter."

It hadn't even been a week since Adam was born. I had a son and a daughter just five days apart. It was hard to wrap my brain around. Life couldn't really get more complicated.

I found my daughter in the nursery. As I looked at the pink card attached to her bassinet, I thought about her name. I would name her Penelope. It was inspired by one of my favorite songs.

She was beautiful. Her little fists waved in the air, and her tiny feet wriggled inside a fleecy onesie. She had a smear of curly black hair on the top of her head. She looked quite a lot like Sam did when she was a newborn.

19

505

By the fall of 1994 an unbelievable amount of money was passing
through our hands. I looked around the office at the stacks of bills
on every table and in every corner. We needed more counting
machines and more men to run them. It was hard to believe how
much had changed for me since that first day I had hesitantly
pushed through the doors and begun my criminal career.

Beep, beep, beep. I checked the new message on my beeper.
It was Dante. 505.

Emergencies were rare. Whatever had happened, it wasn't good.
I flipped open my phone and dialed Dante's number, my blood pressure spiking. "Emilio's in the hospital." Dante's voice quavered.

"In the hospital" was our code for "arrested." The police had
gotten him. It felt like a punch in the gut. "Do you know any more
details?"

There was silence for a moment. "We'll talk." The line went
dead.

Dante was shaken too.

I dropped what I was doing and ran from the building to our
secure contact point.

Dante was pacing when I got there. "It's gonna hit the news. . . .
This one's big."

"How'd he get caught? Where was he?"
Dante shrugged.

We switched on a bulky old radio and tuned it to 1010 WINS. "A major drug bust near Bayside, Queens. More than seventy-two kilograms of cocaine have been seized along with more than two million dollars in small bills."

Expletives burst from my mouth.

There were a lot of drug busts at the time, and they frequently hit the news, but this one was huge. That was going to put a serious dent in our business.

We looked at each other, helpless. Not only could we do nothing to help our brother, but both of us were in serious danger of getting caught.

"I'll let the guys know, and then I'm going home. . . . Don't go to the office right now."

I nodded. There was no way I wanted to step foot near our office. For all I knew, the police were already there.

"And stay off the phone."

I nodded again. I would get information about Emilio from Mami. She'd know what was happening.

Before I left the city, I got news that my brother had been released on bail. I could only imagine how much it must have cost him. His hearing, held at the Kew Gardens Courthouse, was relatively short. His lawyer had found a way to have him released on a technicality.

Fear, frustration, and sadness battled for control of my mind. Normally Samantha and Adam were a great distraction, but even as they giggled and played near my feet, I couldn't shake the thought of Emilio handcuffed in the back of a police car.

Alexandra joined me in the living room with the children, a vague look of annoyance on her face. Or maybe anger.

"Are we going to talk about this? Or do we keep pretending?" Definitely anger.

"He's out on bail. I think he's—"

"That's not what I mean." Her tone was a deadly combination of ice and fire. "I'm talking about what it's doing to us. You're going to end up just like Emilio, if you don't end up dead first. You're ruining our family. You've destroyed my dreams for any sort of normal life!"

She was shouting now, pacing near my chair. Months and years of frustrations, rarely voiced, came spilling out. "My life's become a nightmare! While you're out partying and hanging out at clubs, I am home taking care of our children. When I took Sam camping with my sister's family, all I could think about was how much I wished you were there. How great it would be if my husband wanted to live with me. What it would be like if you wanted me instead of all those other women. Oh yeah, I know about them. You think I don't?"

My already churning insides felt as if they were being torn apart. I rarely thought about how my lifestyle impacted Alexandra, but I couldn't avoid it today. "Baby, baby . . . don't. You're my wife. It's you I love. They're nobodies off the street. You are it. You. Only you." I got up and wrapped my arms around her.

She began to cry. Deep, racking sobs. "I am in hell!" she wailed.

My heart ached for her. But I didn't know what to do. Did she expect me to just find a normal office job? There was no way I could give up the business. It was what I knew, and I was good at it.

It was ages before I contacted Emilio again.

He was making preparations for his exodus. "The NYPD are building their case. Make sure you're careful."

He didn't need to say it. I made sure, when I got back to the city, that my movements weren't being tracked. We drove older, inexpensive vehicles and parked far away from the houses and apartments where we conducted our illegal enterprise. On occasion, we stashed money and drugs at a friend's house. He wasn't involved with our business, but his place was close to the highway and the airport, making it the perfect place to run things from. He was a great sidekick. In time, Dante and I managed to regain much of what we had lost. Life got back on track.

20

BUSTED

My head felt fuzzy from a night of partying. In fact, a strong lethargy had settled over me during the last few months, and I couldn't shake it. My clothes fit a little tighter now, and a long flight of stairs winded me. I ran a hand through my closely cropped hair. I really didn't feel like counting money today.

My beeper chirped. It was a code from Dante telling me he wanted to meet at a friend's place in College Point where we'd stashed some drugs.

I grabbed my jacket and headed for the door. A chill breeze had picked up, flinging debris into the air. I braced myself against it even as I welcomed the cool air that took the edge off of my headache.

Dante was loading several kilos of coke into a duffel bag when I arrived. "It's a big drop today. A new guy. He wants twenty-five kilos. We need to take it near the Plaza Hotel, by Central Park."

Dante stashed six kilos of cocaine in the trunk of a brand-new Mercedes-Benz 600 SL to bring to another client later. I then helped him pack the twenty-five kilos into another duffel bag and load it into the trunk of an Oldsmobile. The plan was to drive to the client and exchange vehicles with him.

As usual, we had one of our guys, Oscar Perez, drive a decoy vehicle. We drove the Oldsmobile over the bridge to Manhattan with no clue whatsoever that the Tactical Narcotics Team had been monitoring our activities for a long time now.

The decoy was just ahead of us. In the driver's seat, I glanced at the rearview mirror; a vehicle with dark windows was hanging a couple of car lengths back but keeping pace. It could be a tail.

I sped up and got on the highway heading west toward the city. The dark-windowed car was still following.

"Let's take I-495," Dante suggested.

A commercial highway, Interstate 495 would allow us to blend in with traffic.

I turned the wheel sharply, cut into the center lane, then sped up and cut back again. I looked behind us. If we were being tailed we'd lost them.

I exhaled, relaxing back against the headrest. I turned off the interstate and headed for the Queensboro Bridge. We came to a red light, and there were twelve or so vehicles in front of us. I craned my head to look back, nervous that we may have picked up that tail again.

Dante swore and pointed at a roadblock ahead.

There was a regular patrol car, and officers were checking every vehicle. We knew they had to be looking for us.

Dante looked my way, and I saw he was ready to run.

I yanked open the door and took off at a sprint without looking back to see which way Dante had gone. I had barely cleared traffic when I heard the shouts of the officers as they gave chase. My lungs already burned, and my legs felt heavy. I had to push through.

LaGuardia Community College was straight ahead. If I could just make it across the street and onto the grounds, I could hide among the mass of students. My side cramped, but I pressed on, cursing the toll partying had taken on my body.

I had made it about three blocks when I felt a hand grab my shoulder. I yanked forward as I ran, and the officer lost his grip.

I shot a look over my shoulder to gauge my distance from the officers. I couldn't run much longer, but they hadn't even broken a sweat. What was the point of running if I had no chance of escape? I slowed down.

They knocked me to the ground. My lungs deflated, and I struggled to inhale. Sweat dripped from my face onto the pavement. *This can't be real. How can this be happening?*

One officer yanked my arms behind my back. There was a metallic *click* as the heavy metal cuffs locked in place around my wrists. His arm across my back ground my shoulders into the pavement.

They yanked me up and led me to the same car that had been following us earlier. We'd been set up.

From my seat in the back of the cop car, I saw them put Dante and Oscar, both handcuffed, into one of the police cars.

The drive went by in a blink. My mind swirled with images of my imminent imprisonment and a heartbroken Alexandra crying out that I had destroyed our family.

I knew I was going to jail. I was guilty of crimes that could put me behind bars for a very long time. But what would happen to my children? There were three little ones who relied on me to put food in their bellies. What if the authorities put a freeze on our accounts?

They led us into a stark room to await processing and tried to interview us. "I'll remind you, Mr. Mendoza, it will be easier for you if you cooperate."

Dante and I had prepared for this ever since Emilio's arrest.

"We won't say anything until our representative from Kenneth Schreiber and Associates is present." Our statement was clear and to the point, and it successfully ended the interrogations.

Mr. Schreiber and his associates didn't offer us any false hope. "Honestly, gentlemen, it's not going to be easy. The number of drug-related cases right now. . . . You've seen the headlines. 'The war on drugs.' The whole climate is going to make it harder to get a favorable verdict."

As expected, the presiding judge denied bail. We were remanded and sent back to a unit in the Queens Detention Center, a prototypical remand center with floor after floor of gray stone and heavy ironwork in place of windows. One good thing about the place was the access to news on the outside. I picked up a copy of the paper;

emblazoned across the front page just under "March 20, 1996," was the headline: "3 Held in $3.8M Drug Bust."

I was curious how much they had gotten right, so I skimmed the first few paragraphs.

They mentioned finding twenty-five kilos of cocaine. That was right.

They had spelled our names correctly.

It said we had been stopped in Long Island City for running a red light. Well, that was news to me. I couldn't help but chuckle. Apparently the district attorney told the media a different story than I remembered. He said that when the cops pulled us over they discovered the drugs. Apparently spewing lies to the reporters wasn't a crime.

I read on. The article said six additional kilos were found at our friend's place. I swore.

If this was what they were telling the press, what else did they have on us?

I read on, *Charged with possessing $3.8 million in cocaine that could get them life in prison.*

My heart began to jackhammer against my ribs. *Life?*

My mind flashed back to my time in Spofford. That had been hell, and I was younger and fitter back then. What would happen to me now? What would happen to my family? I shook my head, trying to shake the feeling of gloom. *We have great lawyers—they will figure out a way to get us out on bail. Right?*

I folded the scratchy blanket on my cot. During the last three months, I had managed to make my dilapidated six-by-nine-foot cell into a slightly less hostile environment than it had been when I arrived.

I'd gotten my hands on some extra blankets to cushion the hard, worn-out mattress. Alexandra, Mami, and Papi all visited me for comfort and support. And when we could, Dante and I would meet up to work out, and we did our best to keep a positive perspective.

"It's that dude Giuliani's fault," I grunted as I hefted some serious poundage up and over my head. "He's asking for it, getting all up in our business."

"I can't stand him," Dante agreed. "I didn't like him when he was the US attorney for the SDNY . . . but now that he's the mayor, I don't like him even more."

Before becoming a mayor, Rudy Giuliani gained national attention for prosecuting high profile cases of mob organizations and big-time drug dealers. The odds were not in our favor.

I dropped the barbell on the ground and wiped the sweat from the back of my neck before it could trail its way down my spine. If we were going to beat this rap, I was going to need to work out much more than my biceps. I had nothing but time, so I decided I might as well work on my legal education.

21

DEAL

My attorney, Mr. Kenneth Schreiber, straightened the cuffs on his impeccable suit before looking up to meet my eyes. His face was somber. I felt the muscles in my shoulders and chest tense.

"How are you holding up, Mr. Mendoza?"

I licked my lips, my mouth suddenly dry. "I'm okay."

I wasn't. I felt nauseated. I knew I couldn't expect good news. I steeled myself for the worst. *At least we can get some closure.* The months of waiting to be sentenced seemed almost worse than the sentence itself.

He nodded, but it was clear the question was a matter of politeness and my response barely registered.

"The assistant DA has come back with a plea option."

I leaned toward him, all ears.

"Three to nine years with the possibility of parole after three years with good behavior and six years of parole supervision!"

I could feel the tension release between my shoulder blades. Dante and I had both been expecting the mandatory fifteen- to twenty-five-year sentence.

Mr. Schreiber smiled. "It's good news, isn't it?" He put a stack of papers on the table between us. "It looks like you were right, Herman. The police used racial profiling. It seems like stops and searches were done specifically for people of Hispanic descent. Especially those with high-end vehicles. As you and Dante were parked at the red light and hadn't committed any traffic violations"—he flipped through some more papers—"there was nothing in your situation that justified the police pulling you over and searching your vehicle."

I couldn't stop nodding and grinning. It was almost more than I could comprehend.

"And I have more good news."

More good news? I didn't think it could get much better.

"You are eligible for the Shock Program."

He tapped his pen on his notepad, obviously pleased with the work he had done on our behalf.

"What is, uh . . ." I cleared my throat, an unexpected tightness building.

"What's Shock?"

I nodded.

"A substitute for prison time. You're only eligible because you're a first-time offender. In a nutshell, it's a six-month incarcerated rehabilitation program."

"Six months?" I was sure he had mentioned a minimum incarceration of three years.

"That's right. Because the program is meant to rehabilitate rather than merely punish an offense, if you complete the program, you won't have to serve the remainder of the sentence. It creates a strict routine of discipline, intensive regimentation, exercise, and work therapy along with substance abuse treatment, education, and counseling."

It took a minute for his words to sink in. Compared to years in prison, it sounded like paradise. I was so grateful I could have cried. "Did Dante get the same?"

Mr. Schreiber shook his head, the grim look returning to his face.

"I'm afraid not. Given his position as head of the organization, they're offering four to twelve years of incarceration."

A sudden sense of loss cut into my joy.

"They've been investigating Dante for quite some time, and they've compiled a lot more evidence against him."

Even so, it was a better outcome than we had expected considering the amount of drugs seized.

"Mendoza!"

I woke with a start at the sound of my name. Today was my sentencing. I glanced at the clock. It was 5:00 A.M. It was a ridiculously early start to the day, but I was eager to get on with it.

Two guards entered my cell, slapped handcuffs on me, and led me to the bullpen to wait.

The bullpen was as cold and dank as the bleakest dungeon—like something you'd see in a movie. Dozens of inmates welcomed me with snarls and glares. There was a whole different kind of criminal in the bullpen. Filth emanated in waves off the drunks and vagrants they had brought in off the streets: urine, mold, stale beer, and whatever else they had rolled in. To make matters worse, there was only one exposed toilet. Most didn't even try to aim. Even after my three months in the housing unit, the bullpen felt like a new low. At least in the unit I had a cell with a bed.

I was tired, and I desperately wanted to sleep, but one glance at the stained cement floor told me I was better off standing. I found an open space at the bars of the pen and leaned against them, shutting my eyes against my repulsive surroundings.

"Do you accept the terms of the plea agreement?" the judge asked.

I glanced at my family seated several feet away, hope brightening their eyes.

"I do, Your Honor."

That was it. That was all that needed to be heard.

The judge raised his gavel. "I hereby sentence you to three to nine years of incarceration, as agreed upon by the prosecution."

Bang!

The breath I had been holding escaped the moment the gavel hit the block. Three long months of uncertainty had come to an end.

22

SENT TO PRISON

I didn't think anything could be worse than the bullpen, but my first month on Rikers Island changed my mind. Sure, the food here was a small step up, and I wasn't sharing a space with people who soiled themselves repeatedly, but this jail was full of actual lunatics. I was scared for my life.

It wasn't the kind of place designed to help mentally disturbed people either. I was so bored I often wondered if I would go crazy myself. The only thing I had to occupy my time was exercise. A hundred push-ups each day. This had benefits, of course. In the last week I had noticed a marked improvement in my strength. The puffiness in my face and gut disappeared. I had started to look like I could survive this place.

Rikers Island had ten jails and housed more than fourteen thousand inmates, many of whom had gang affiliations. Everywhere I looked I could see gang colors; some I recognized and some I didn't. The guy with the facial tattoos and the red bandana in his back pocket had to be a Blood. The guys across the yard sporting blue and looking like they were about to destroy the Asian guy with the comb-over had to be Crips. Most of the Puerto Ricans looked like they belonged to the Ñetas, and I recognized the Latin Kings, but there were masses more I couldn't identify.

"Herman. Wanna spot me?" It was Dante.

I nodded and followed him to the weights, my eyes constantly scanning our surroundings. You had to be vigilant when you were in the yard. At any moment, things could go south and you could end up with a homemade shiv in your gut.

"Did you hear what happened in the cafeteria?" I asked him.

"Yeah. Glad I missed it. Was it the Latin Kings?"

"They started it, but it was the Crips that came out on top."

"How many did they lose?" he asked, lying back on the bench.

"Two. But they both have guys in the infirmary."

I loaded more weight onto the barbell and glanced around, still on edge.

"Man, we gotta just keep our heads down," he said.

When Dante finished his set, we traded places. I was grateful he was not only in the same prison, but in the same unit as I was.

"Did they say when you're going to Shock?"

"No," I grunted, holding the heavy weight high above my head. "But I'm gonna be ready."

From Rikers Island, Dante and I were transferred to Ulster Correctional Facility without any word on when I would be relocated. I was getting nervous that it might be years before it happened. It would be strange to move to a new place without Dante, though. We'd been lucky to have each other. Without Dante I'd have no one to watch my back.

Then one day, after I had settled into Ulster, a corrections officer stopped at the door to my cell. "Three five seven six!" He guided me to a waiting pen.

I was handed off to another officer, who stood with shackles in hand. I offered him my wrists, and an all-too-familiar weight settled around them. Without being asked, I spread my legs shoulder width apart so that he could shackle my ankles. The metal pressed into my heavy boots, rubbing against bone. I was marched forward to a van. I was on my way to Shock.

23

SHOCK

By the end of our two-hour drive, I had almost convinced myself that the next six months wouldn't be so bad. I had heard that Shock was like a military boot camp on steroids, but it couldn't be any worse than prison, could it?

Outside the large barrack-style facility, officers in gray were lined up and waiting.

My feet had barely touched the gray gravel when a drill officer began to bark orders. "Get your bags, ya lousy ingrates!"

I glanced up, feeling I should acknowledge the man shouting the instructions. That was a mistake.

"Eyes front!"

I snapped my gaze forward.

"Everything from today on will be 'Yes, sir' or 'No, sir.' You will speak only when spoken to."

There was a pause. It took a second before I realized we were meant to respond.

"Yes, sir!" I shouted. My voice was less firm, less in-control than I expected.

"March!"

We marched.

———

I was assigned to a platoon with about forty other guys. Many of them looked as if they'd have difficulty completing any task more arduous than making their beds.

"This is your daily itinerary!"

One of our drill instructors held up a copy of the paper they had just passed around. "Study it. Learn it."

I looked down at the paper in my hands.

5:00 A.M.—Wake-Up Call Followed by Inspection

I groaned. We not only had to be awake by 5:00 A.M., but we needed to be dressed and have our beds made in military fashion before the drill instructor arrived.

"Tardiness will not be tolerated!" Our drill instructor's eyes narrowed as he scanned our faces.

A guy at the end of the room raised his hand.

The instructor marched down the line and shoved his face less than an inch from the other guy. "Something you don't understand, maggot?"

The inmate shrank back, visibly intimidated by this ex-marine. The instructor smiled, baring his teeth. "I didn't think so."

Five o'clock came awfully early the next morning. I scrambled off my cot, pulled on my uniform, and laced up my boots.

I pulled the sheet tight across my bed, folded my blanket, and arranged my pillow. I thought I had moved superhumanly fast, but there were several guys who stood in parade rest beside their sharply made beds before I was done.

Inspection took longer than I expected. The instructor managed to find fault with beds or uniforms that I thought looked perfectly fine.

"You can't make a bed, maggot? Your mommy always do that for you? Still need her to change your diaper too?" he screamed at the guy across from me, tearing his blanket from the bed and shoving it into his arms. "Do it again. And give me a hundred push-ups."

When inspection finally ended, we marched outside for physical training.

My preparation in Rikers and Ulster had helped. If I'd come here straight after my arrest, I might not have survived. In the morning alone we did hundreds of jumping jacks and push-ups followed by a two-mile run.

A couple of guys at the back of the line were crying, stumbling forward, barely able to stay on their feet. My own breath came in short, fiery gasps. My muscles and joints ached. Sweat poured down my face and wet the back of my shirt. I licked at my upper lip. I was so parched that even the salty moisture on my skin tasted good.

By evening, two of the guys from my platoon were missing.

"What happened to Williams and Sanchez?" we asked the instructor at the end of the day.

He shook his head. "They're heading back to prison. They opted to serve out their sentences rather than try to complete the program."

I couldn't understand their decision. It was a hard day—I understood that—but why on earth would you voluntarily return to prison for three more years when there was a chance to get out in six months?

"Hey, dummy!"

Several of us in the dormitory turned around. The instructor really could be talking to any of us.

Our instructor stormed over to a short, wiry man whose triangular eyebrows made him appear perpetually surprised. "You can't follow directions? No talking means no talking!"

The command was followed by a string of obscenities and a spray of spittle in the little man's face. He blinked and wiped at his cheek, further angering the instructor.

The drill instructor stormed off only to return a minute later with a roll of tape and a piece of paper that read, *I'm a dummy that can't follow orders.* The instructor slapped a piece of tape across the man's mouth and made him tape the sign to the front of his shirt.

He was trying to establish a sense of discipline and self-control in us. If we followed orders to the letter, our proclivity toward impulsiveness would slowly be weeded out of us.

As I lay in my cot that night, and the snores of my bunkmates filled the air, I almost cried. I tried to swallow the enormous lump in my throat, but it wouldn't shift. Boot camp was harder than I'd expected. I'd thought Shock sounded like paradise compared to three years in prison, but I'd been wrong. Those boring days lifting weights in the yard with Dante were a breeze compared to this. But if I quit and went back to prison, Samantha, Adam, and Penelope would be in school by the time I got out.

I sat up straight and shook my head. *I will not give up!*

After five months of hell camp and its regimented schedule, I broke. I needed some sort of divine intervention if I was going to finish Shock. I pulled on my boots and headed for the chapel.

I believed in God—kinda. I figured it was at least worth asking for the big guy's help to get through this.

Although the chapel wasn't more than thirty square feet, the room felt cavernous. Its wooden pews were mostly empty, since there was only a handful of inmates inside. I felt awkward as soon as I entered. I thought about sitting down, but my legs refused to move any farther. This would have to do. I leaned against the back wall and closed my eyes. "Lord," I prayed, "if I pass this program, I promise I won't drink alcohol for six months. Not one drop."

I thought that promise should impress Him. Six months was a long time, and He knew how much I loved my Johnnie Walker.

December 23, 1996, the last morning of the Shock Incarceration Program, dawned cold and gray. The few remaining members of our platoon had one last hurdle to jump before we could graduate—a military-style drill with several formations performed in front of our loved ones.

My joints ached with each swing of my arm and each stomp of my foot, but I had to keep focused. I just needed to stay in line with the others . . . but no matter how fast we marched, my muscles refused to warm up and cooperate.

Icy winds stole my breath. I tried to inhale deeply, but it only made my lungs burn and my throat feel dry. My whole body shook from the cold.

Somewhere on the premises, in the seats reserved for our families, Alexandra sat. Even while one part of my brain screamed at me to give up, turn back to the barracks, and get under a blanket, the sensible part reminded me that I had come so far. It was lunacy to quit now.

I took another step. Measured. Precise.

I'm getting closer to Alexandra.

Another step. *Just finish it.*

Another. *I am a different guy than I was when I walked in here.*

Another. *I'll get to see the kids again.*

I felt every bone in my foot as I planted my boot on icy, packed earth.

I am disciplined. I am not a maggot. I am not an idiot.

Another step, another swing of the arm. *I won't wimp out now. The end is close. My platoon is beside me. We're in this together.*

Fifty meters left—we could make it.

Ten meters.

A cheer erupted as we crossed the finish line and were ushered to our graduation ceremony.

I was bone tired, but the weariness and the shaking had eased. I looked for Alexandra in the sea of visiting faces. *What if she hadn't come? What if she decided to leave me? What if—*

Her little wave caught my attention, and I grinned. *I knew she would come.*

"Herman Mendoza."

They called my name! I had done it.

"We commend you for your determination and resilience. Congratulations on completing the Shock Program."

I tried to appear solemn and serious as I accepted my certificate, but I couldn't contain my joy. With those words, I was released back into society.

Alexandra met me at the doors. She opened up her arms, and I ran into them, first squeezing her and then kissing her. I had almost forgotten how sweet her kisses were.

"Ready?"

I nodded.   •

Her voice wasn't as warm as I had remembered. Was that wariness I heard? I would have to prove to her that I really was a changed man.

She pointed to her car across the parking lot. "I'm just over there."

Alexandra drove in silence for a few minutes, glancing over at me every few seconds, as if I were an apparition that might disappear again at any moment. There was so much to say, so much to catch up on. Almost too much. We didn't know where to begin.

We were almost to the city when Alexandra interrupted our small talk with something more serious. "Don't expect much when we get there. We've lost almost everything in legal fees."

"It can't all have gone to legal fees."

"Not all of it . . . but there were some family obligations too."

I cursed under my breath.

She put a hand on my arm. "It's going to be a fresh start."

I nodded. We could handle it. At least it was better than prison time.

"The kids and I moved into my sister's place, so we could make ends meet."

My heart sunk a little. I understood why she had rented out our home for extra income, but I had been looking forward to being at home with my wife. We needed time together to fix some big issues.

24

Six-Month Promise

The parole office in Jamaica, Queens, was full of seedy-looking criminals. Its waiting room was a vast space filled with airport-style seating. I wiped dust from the side of my dark dress pants. The others here had obviously not run an organization like I had. There was no level of sophistication about them. They wore their hair greasy and unkempt. Most were ravaged by the effects of drugs, their skin pockmarked and mutilated. Scars warned that they were fighters, and gang tattoos told you who had their backs.

An officer stepped into the waiting area with a stack of papers in his hand. He looked like a real hard case. "Herman Mendoza?"

I shot up from my seat. He gestured for me to follow him to a locked door where we were buzzed through. He escorted me inside his office and explained the requirements I was expected to follow.

"If you don't follow them to the letter, you'll be in violation of your parole and will be sent back to prison."

I nodded. I'd just gotten my life back; I had no intention of violating anything.

"You'll have to find a job, and I want to see paper work from your employer."

I nodded again.

"There will be random drug testing—"

"That's not going to be an issue." The weekly humiliation of providing an observed urine sample was a small price to pay for my freedom.

He rolled his eyes at my assurances and shoved a piece of paper across the desk. "This is your weekly schedule."

I wiped my clammy palms on my black suit pants, ready for the inevitable handshake. I'd had no qualms about checking *no* when the job application asked if I had ever been convicted of a crime. If I had said yes, I would have never gotten this interview, but it wouldn't take much digging on their part to find out the truth.

Don't worry, I told myself. *You've got loads of experience selling . . . sales is sales.*

There weren't many jobs that fit my particular skill set, and there were even fewer that could sustain my family. So when my search of the classifieds turned up this opportunity to work as a sales rep for a sorbet company, I knew I needed to give it my best shot.

"Mr. Mendoza?"

I plastered a smile on my face, ready to charm my potential employer.

I took a seat at the conference table, purposefully resting my arms on the armrests instead of clutching them in my lap. Across from me sat not only the man who had called me in, but two other company executives, all wearing dark suits and polite expressions.

The man in the middle glanced down at my application form. "Tell us about yourself, Herman."

I waited just a second before speaking, not because I didn't know what to say, but because I wanted to give the appearance of calm control. "As you can see, I've been in sales for a number of years." I was desperate, so I had put fake jobs on my application.

They nodded.

"I'm a people person. I like getting to know my clients and helping them find a product that is right for them."

The moment the men relaxed and leaned in, I could see that they were impressed. When they'd finished with their questions, the one who had called me in said, "We'll give you a call."

Did that mean I had the job? It seemed like it, but I didn't want to get my hopes up.

I momentarily thought about celebrating with a drink, but the weight of the promise I had made to God in the Shock chapel came back to me. I still had a few months left on that contract.

———

The phone rang just after supper that night, and I knew before I even picked it up that it would be the sorbet company.

"Hello. Mr. Mendoza?"

"Yes?"

"The job is yours! Can you start Monday?"

I fist-pumped the air and gave a silent squeal. It was my first legitimate job in years. It felt good.

It turns out selling sorbet isn't massively different from selling drugs. The principles of sales are still the same. Each day I went to the offices at the top floor of the factory and collected samples, which were packed in a bucket of dry ice. The owners then handed me a list of leads and potential customers. I would visit various restaurants and shops and present the product.

When I was selling cocaine, I would spend countless hours in restaurants meeting clients. This meant that I was already on friendly terms with a number of restaurant owners. Most of them had no idea what business I had been in. These contacts helped me to open loads of new accounts in top restaurant chains. I was climbing the ladder of success.

"You'll never guess who I got a meeting with," I said to one of the owners of my company one day.

"This is why you're my top guy." He grinned. "Who is it?"

"Just the owner of one of the most prestigious restaurants in New York City."

When I told him the name I could see the surprise creep over his face, tugging his eyebrows up toward his receding hairline. He clapped me on the shoulder. "Herman! Nicely done. That's huge. When do you meet him? I'll join you."

It wasn't a request. Nailing that account could bring in some big revenue. It wasn't that he didn't trust me to manage it—he just wanted to be there for what could be the signing of their biggest account.

We walked in together, and I got that same feeling I used to get when Dante and I made a big sale. Surprisingly, my boss let me initiate the pitch. I smiled and charmed, complimenting the restaurant owner on his fine taste and his success. I presented samples and talked about how each might complement their menu. By the end, I had not only gained a new account, but also the respect of my boss.

"You did good, Herman," he said as we drove back to the warehouse together. "I knew there was a reason we needed to hire you."

I couldn't help but feel proud, and I could see that I had made him proud as well. I didn't want to screw it up, but the boss and I had started to become friends. I thought maybe I should come clean about my past. My pulse jumped a little as I broached the subject. "I was pretty relieved when you did. I have to admit, I wasn't entirely honest on my application."

He glanced over at me, curious.

I shifted in my seat. "Actually, I had just recently gotten out of prison when I applied."

He cursed. Not in anger, but in surprise. "You're kidding me!"

"I wish I was."

He cursed again, then chuckled. "Well, I guess I'm glad you lied . . . because you turned out to be one of our best guys."

I hadn't realized quite how nervous I was to tell him until the tension eased. He was fine with it. I was fine. In six months, I had turned my life around. Six months! That also meant my promise to God was fulfilled. It had been a long time without a drink.

25

A Dog Returns to Its Vomit

Within six months of my completing Shock, things were looking pretty good. By this point I had resumed my weekend commutes to the Poconos. Alexandra had moved back into our house, and I had moved right back in with Daria.

I had a lot to celebrate. Not only was my life back on track, but I had kept my promise to God. For the half year I had given up alcohol, there wasn't a day that went by that I didn't wish I could toss back a shot of Jack with friends, or sip a nice Chardonnay with a big plate of pasta in front of me. I was itching for a drink. I searched my brain for someone I could celebrate my freedom with. Alexandra was out of the running. She wouldn't approve. But maybe my friend Rolando . . .

Rolando Castile and I were very close. Ours was a work friendship. He was the human equivalent of a grizzly bear and the man I called whenever I needed backup on a drug deal.

I dialed his number.

"Yeah?" his gruff voice barked.

"Rolando! What are you up to tonight? Wanna drink?"

"Always."

I chuckled. I knew I could count on him. Rolando was an expert drinker, and in that way, we were like blood brothers. I suggested a place I knew that was famous for its fine dining and hip young regulars.

It was strange drinking with Rolando. Clinking glass after glass and chatting about mutual acquaintances, as if no time had passed and it was any typical Friday night.

We were a few drinks in when I spotted a familiar face at the bar. Andreas.

His uncle was the head of the Colombian cartel, the same organization I had worked with before. I quickly looked away, pretending not to see him. I wasn't keen to reacquaint myself with him, but I wasn't going to be rude and make an enemy of him either. I focused hard on Rolando's wide face as he spoke, suddenly unable to follow the conversation.

I heard footsteps come up beside me. "Hey, Herman! ¿Qué pasa? ¿Cómo estás?" Andreas slugged my arm in a friendly greeting.

I turned, affecting a look of pleased surprise. "Andreas! Hi! How you doing? It's been a long time."

He grinned. "Yeah, I heard you got incarcerated."

I shrugged. "I'm out now."

I tried to smile, but my pulse was hammering. Rolando must have sensed my discomfort, because he shifted in his seat, drawing Andreas's attention.

"Sorry, man. I didn't realize you were here with anyone." He nodded a greeting to Rolando, who responded in kind.

"Do you mind if I just have a word with Herman? It's been a long time."

A thousand curses filled my mind as I followed him to the back of the restaurant. "What are you up to these days? Are you back in business?"

"Naw, man. I'm all legit now, selling sorbet. What are you up to?" I didn't want to ask. But I didn't want him to think I was avoiding him either. At the time of my arrest, Andreas had been in charge of distribution for the cartel. He was a powerful man with powerful connections.

"I gotta tell you man, business is booming. My uncle's in Cali right now. It's a prime location. He's got me moving over a ton of coke all through the Eastern Seaboard."

The jackhammering in my rib cage increased. *Is he offering me an in?* I listened as he detailed the success of their operation, and then he said it.

"You let me know whenever you need work." In other words, he would provide as much cocaine as I wanted. "I can even give it to you on credit. A million's worth, two million, whatever you want."

My conscience screamed at me not to do it. Selling sorbet paid the bills, and I was pretty decent at it. *But I will never make the kind of dough I can selling coke.*

If Alexandra found out that I had gotten back into the business, it would destroy her. And it was dangerous. And I had the kids to think about. "Thanks, man, but I'm doing really great selling sorbet."

As soon as the words left my mouth I felt relieved. My conscience had been battling hard—it deserved this win. I had to get back to Rolando quickly. If I didn't, I would cave. I congratulated Andreas on his success and said a friendly good-bye.

I sat back down beside my friend with a heavy sigh. He shifted his bulky, six-foot frame on the skinny bar stool and leaned close. "What was that all about?"

I shook my head. "You won't believe it. That was my old friend, Andreas. His uncle is the head of the Colombian cartel, and he was offering to front me a couple mills' worth of coke."

If Rolando were a cartoon character, there would have been dollar signs scrolling across his eyes and a jackpot sign blinking above his head. He could barely sit still in his chair. "Just like old times, man! Why don't you let me move that work? I'll work for you, and all you gotta do is count your money."

Greed crept through my veins, fighting my conscience for ownership of my heart. Heat washed through me, in response to the increase in my heart rate.

I spotted Andreas nearby and walked up to him. "Let's do this."

Andreas grinned and held out his hand. I shook it, firming my resolve.

"How much do you need?"

"It's been a while. Why not give me ten kilos to start?"

And just like that, I was back in.

26

MINDING MY OWN BEESWAX

"Two fifty. Piece of cake." Rolando dropped a duffel bag onto the table between us.

"How was Connecticut?"

Rolando had an apartment and connections in Connecticut and had taken the coke there to sell.

"Hungry for it."

I grinned. Though $250,000 wasn't as big of a haul as I made before my incarceration, it was nothing to sneeze at. In just over twenty-four hours we had made a quick and tidy profit of $55,000. I counted out $15,000 and handed it to Rolando, keeping $40,000 for myself. I made forty grand just by having the right connections.

I wasn't going to get in as deep as I did before. If I kept this up, I could make as much as $220,000 a month. I planned to stop as soon as I had a decent nest egg to retire on.

"Hey, Herman!"

My brother Fabian waved to me from the door of my parents' house, his face grave.

I had just spent ten minutes circling the block to find a parking space and was feeling annoyed. I trudged up the walk to the front step. "What?"

"They got Emilio."

I stopped walking, my mouth ajar. I knew Emilio and his family were back. They had settled down in Miami under assumed names. I didn't contact them very often, because I didn't want to put him in any danger.

"When?" I had a lot of questions, but I doubted Fabian had the answers.

"Yesterday morning. They're bringing him back here tomorrow. Mami's pretty upset, so if you want to talk about it, do it out here."

"Do you know how they got him?"

"The guy that turned him in was a business acquaintance. He knew about Emilio's past, and when he got arrested, he told the cops where to find Emilio so that they'd go easy on him."

I cursed the rat. He probably got a great deal—reduced his own jail time. Emilio had likely made some mistakes as well. He, like most people, was a creature of habit.

"They picked him up outside his gym."

I muttered another curse even as my brain shifted into planning mode. "I'll call our lawyer. Maybe we can get him out on bail."

Fabian nodded, his face like concrete. He and Gabriel hated getting involved in what Emilio, Dante, and I were up to. In their eyes, we were a constant disappointment.

Bail wouldn't be an easy thing to get, since Emilio had failed to appear in court before. I squeezed Fabian's shoulder as I stepped past him into the house. There were no familiar, homey smells emanating from the kitchen. Mami was on the sofa in the living room, crying.

It took a little time for Mr. Schreiber to negotiate Emilio's bail. The only way he would get out was if we came up with a half million.

"Por favor, hijo," Mami cried, "usa mi casa."

I didn't want to use my parents' house as collateral, but I couldn't refuse Mami anything. She was in a delicate state. For the next few days, she refused to leave the house, and when any of us checked on her she was always on her bed, curled in a fetal position, screaming, "¡Dios, ten piedad! God, have mercy!" and sobbing.

As much as possible, Gabriel and Fabian kept their distance. The world Emilio and I lived in frightened them. They didn't want to get involved. They were afraid for us as much as they were embarrassed by us.

It took three weeks to verify that the property was not purchased with ill-gotten gains, but after that, the judge approved bail and Emilio was released.

Emilio met me after the trial, grabbed me up in a bear hug, and slapped my back enthusiastically.

"How have you been? Did this whole mess take you away from work?"

I shook my head. "I met up with Andreas a little while back, and he set me up. I'm back in business. It's making a tidy profit, if you want in. . . ."

I let the words hang there for a minute. I didn't want to push Emilio into anything, but we had made a good team in the past.

He slapped his leg in glee. "If we handle it right, we could make millions in no time! We could retire early. Leave the States behind and start fresh."

Emilio's enthusiasm was contagious. I was glad he was back; Emilio had all sorts of ideas to boost our network. "I know this guy, an old associate of mine. He's got his own trucking company. And each truck is tricked out."

My mind raced at the possibilities. If we could move the drugs outside of New York, we'd be rolling in it. There was high demand for coke outside the city, so the value of each kilo would almost double.

"You talk to John about it?" he asked.

When Emilio was still living in Florida, he'd asked me to contact his drug courier, John. John still owed Emilio a boatload of money. I'd met with him sporadically; his entire company was a front for money laundering and drug sales.

"I did. If we supply, he'll deliver."

Emilio nodded. "Good. I think we can trust him."

In July of 1998, Emilio and I sat inside our new "office" at a local motel's bar, waiting for John. John had passed a test delivery we had given him, so we gave him another four kilos to deliver before meeting us back at the inn.

What made this place ideal was its location in a trendy area of the city right off several major expressways and parkways.

On any given night, you might find Emilio and me at the bar just off the first-floor lobby downing drinks and making deals.

Emilio sat down at the table across from me and tapped on the folder between us. "What you got there?"

I pulled out some pay stubs and paper work emblazoned with my fake construction company's name and logo. I had them made after I quit my legitimate job at the sorbet company. "I told my parole officer I started a business, and he wanted to see the pay stubs and financials."

Emilio smiled and took one of the pay stubs out to examine it. "Nicely done."

I was pretty pleased with how legitimate they all looked.

"Will you be back in time to meet the client?"

"Yeah, seven o'clock?"

Emilio nodded.

I gave him a thumbs-up before tossing back my breakfast Guinness and ordering another. I had started substituting meals with beer, because I knew if I ate as well as I drank, I would be as soft and pudgy as I was before jail.

John walked into the bar with a duffel bag and sat down next to us, dropping the bag on the floor next to my chair. "Here you go."

I nodded and stood. "I'll be back in a minute."

We had booked a room so we would have a place to count the cash. I swung the strap of the duffel bag over my shoulder and sauntered out, spinning the room key on my finger.

John was short several grand. He'd come through for us on delivery, but I was starting to get frustrated. I split the take into three piles, a small one for John and two large stacks for Emilio and me.

Back at the bar, I gave Emilio a nod. He and John had done a few shots while I was gone and were ready to leave. I wasn't so ready to go home. It had been a long, stressful day, and all I wanted was to find a party with some fine women and live it up like I used to.

I found my way to my favorite club. Sidling past the line of people waiting to get in, I gave a nod to the bouncers at the door and headed up to the VIP section.

27

THE TAKEDOWN

I wasn't drunk exactly, but I wasn't fit to drive. It was late on a Friday night, and I had just been to a meeting at an after-hours nightclub. I couldn't trust myself to drive, and taxis were scarce. I was going to have to walk. Not home—there was no point in going home now. But I had a safe house here in Queens that wasn't far away.

Ahead of me, I spotted a couple of guys heading to the parking lot. One of them had to be my old buddy, Oscar. Same build. Same walk.

"Hey, Oscar!" I called. "Can you give me a ride?"

Oscar turned. "Hey, man! Where you headed?"

"Not far."

He waved me over.

"Nice wheels." I ran a hand along the roof of his sedan.

He shrugged. "It's a rental."

Oscar's buddy headed to the passenger's side door, so I headed to the back. I was a little surprised to find another guy sitting back there, but I nodded a greeting and climbed inside.

We had just driven past Thirty-Seventh Avenue and Ninety-Ninth Street in Corona when Oscar suddenly hit the gas. As we were pushed back into our seats by the sudden increase in speed, red and blue lights started flashing behind us, and a siren began to wail.

I glanced out the back window, my heart racing. These streets were tight, and the cops were right on our tail. If they caught us, I was 100 percent certain that they would find a gun in the car. Oscar and his guys almost always packed some sort of heat.

I made a mental list of anything the cops could hold against me. I'd never touched the gun; they wouldn't find my prints on it. Fortunately, this was a rental car. Even if they found anything else, it couldn't be definitively pinned on us.

Oscar made a couple of hard turns, and for a minute it seemed like he'd lost our tail. Then came a sound that stopped my pulse. *Thwup, thwup, thwup, thwup, thwup.*

The cops had a helicopter. It was directly above us. We were screwed.

Oscar slammed on the brakes. The other two passengers cursed, threw open their doors, and took off running. They jumped a wire fence and into a backyard. For the briefest of moments, I considered following them. But I knew that running was incriminating.

Calm down, I told myself. *You've nothing to hide. At least not in the car.*

Within moments, we were surrounded. They had weapons drawn and badges out.

"Get out of the car! Out of the car! Hands up!"

I took a deep breath and slowly opened the door, raising my hands high above my head. Four or five officers swooped in and threw me to the ground. Bright spotlights from the helicopter illuminated the otherwise dark and narrow street. I felt a knee press hard into my back, crushing my ribs against the ground.

"Where's the gun? Where's the gun?" the officer screamed in my ear.

I didn't reply. We would all be okay if Oscar kept his mouth shut.

I tried to lift my head from the cold pavement and called back to Oscar in Spanish, "Don't say anything! They can't pin anything on us. We'll get an attorney."

Oscar must have heard me, because he didn't say a word.

The officer didn't appreciate my outburst. He yanked my arm behind me and slapped a handcuff across my wrist. "Find it?" he called to the other officers.

"Not yet."

I hoped that meant there wasn't one, but it was more likely that Oscar had it well hidden.

"Let's take them in. I'm sure we'll find it," the officer arresting me assured the others.

We pulled up to the 110th precinct and were manhandled into the building.

"We had a complaint that a group of Hispanic men threatened someone with a handgun." The officers questioning me looked me up and down, their eyes accusing and voices threatening.

Play it cool, Herman. Don't try and defend yourself. They'll just twist what you say. Listening to my own wise counsel, I shrugged, responding only with, "I plead the fifth."

The officer threw up his arms in frustration. It was a swift end to the interview.

"Can I call my attorney now?"

Mr. Schreiber got right to work as I waited in the precinct and then in central booking to be arraigned. When he finally sat down across from me to go over the preparations for the trial, it was with good and bad news.

"The bad news is, they found an illegal, fully loaded, semi-automatic handgun well hidden in the trunk of the car you were traveling in. The prosecutor is citing probable cause."

The fact that Mr. Schreiber delivered his bad news with a smile made me think it wouldn't be a big issue.

"The good news is that there was absolutely no evidence that you had any knowledge of an illegal firearm being in the vehicle. You were an innocent passenger on your way home when the police surrounded the vehicle, escalating an otherwise calm situation."

It was true. I had no real knowledge of the gun, just a heavy suspicion that there would be one, because it was Oscar's ride and that was how he rolled.

The judge, after hearing both sides and reviewing the evidence, found there wasn't sufficient evidence to detain me further and ordered my release.

I was home free and feeling mighty proud about it. Even though I didn't actually have anything to do with the gun, my quick thinking on the scene had secured my freedom.

28

BUSTED AGAIN

"John's really been pushing his luck," I muttered.

Emilio nodded. "But he's always come through before."

"Still, it's eighty grand he's shorted us now. And he had the guts to ask for another five kilos. He better not mess us over."

"Relax. He's got a lot more to lose on this deal than we do."

Emilio was right. We stood to make $10,000 per kilo. Once I had our delivery guy, Rolando, drop him another five kilos, John would owe us $200,000. He promised he could get it to us by the end of the week.

True to his word, John called us seven days later. "I'm sorry, man. I couldn't get all of it, but I have fifty G's for you. Where should I drop it?"

I was annoyed, but $50,000 was better than nothing. "Meet me at the Crowne Plaza by LaGuardia."

John strode into the lobby of the Plaza, made the handoff, and walked on. I swung the duffel bag over my shoulder and headed for the room we'd booked.

Emilio was waiting for me there. "Let's count it up."

I unzipped the duffel bag and shook its contents onto the bed. Little stacks of bills landed with a bounce, forming a small pyramid. Emilio and I each grabbed a stack and started counting.

Then I noticed something that stopped my heart. "They're in sequence."

Emilio paused and then flipped through the bills in his hands.

Choice curses burst from our mouths. Numerical sequence was a clear indication that the money was furnished by the police and marked so they could follow the trail. John was a rat.

"That's it. It's over. They know who we are."

I threw the stack of bills I was holding onto the bed and swore again. I was angry at the thought that we were being investigated, but even more furious that John, one of our longest-working employees, had turned out to be an informer.

It struck me then. "We're never getting that $200,000 he owes us."

Emilio shouted another string of obscenities.

"We need to give Andreas a heads-up. If they're on to us, they'll be on to him too."

I texted our supplier in code, and he came to meet me near the hotel. His response was the same as Emilio's and mine. He cursed John out but took his cut of the money anyway.

When the money was split, I was left with twenty grand. Twenty thousand marked bills. I wasn't going to just throw them away. If I could quickly disperse them in a makeshift laundering operation, I could get clean money. I would need it. The cops were probably watching my accounts.

I needed to call Alexandra. I was supposed to be home this weekend, so she would wonder what had happened if I didn't call soon.

"Alexandra, baby. I can't talk long. Things are hot right now."

She knew what that meant without having to ask any questions. "So you aren't coming home. That's what you're saying?"

"Not for a bit."

"Okay. So . . . call me later."

The line went dead before I was ready to hang up. It's not that I wanted to say lots over the phone, but didn't she realize my world was on the brink of falling apart? I could have used some sympathy.

I slept fitfully that night at Daria's place, tossing and turning in semiconsciousness. When light finally filtered through slits in the vertical blinds, I was fully awake, staring at the ceiling with red, bleary eyes, running through scenarios in my head.

Flying internationally would be difficult. Canada and Mexico were clichéd choices but could be my only hope.

I grabbed my cell phone and flipped it open. I tried one of the girls on my speed dial who was usually up for anything. "Hey, Heather. I was just thinking about you. Want to meet me for a drink?"

Life carried on, and slowly Emilio and I felt like we could relax. We started to show up to important deals in person. How much could the cops know, really? It couldn't be much if we were still in business.

Emilio found me in a hotel bar one morning several weeks after we had severed ties with John. "I just got a call. I need to meet a client. Come with me?"

It was late afternoon when Emilio and I crossed over to Manhattan. We pulled into the parking lot where we would meet with the client to discuss drug deals in person. There were other vehicles parked there. Emilio and I scoped the vehicles. None of them raised any red flags.

I had finally gotten over the feeling that someone was watching me. No more alarm bells were going off in my head. Maybe we really were untouchable.

Alexandra had tried to convince me to cut my losses and get out, but she had no idea of the scope and magnitude of our venture. I just needed a few more months, and we could be set for life.

I glanced at my watch. Five more minutes. If the client wasn't there in five minutes, we might have to do another turn around the block.

Suddenly, men in dark jackets poured from four parked cars with tinted windows, guns pointed directly at us.

"DEA! Put your hands where we can see them! Now!"

Adrenaline flooded my system.

On the dashboard was my day planner—a little book listing all our contacts: clients, dealers, and top cartel members. It wasn't large and easily fit into the pocket of my jacket. If the feds got their hands on it and broke the simple code it was written in, it would topple everything. It had to be protected. I fumbled around for a place to stuff it. When I was satisfied it was safe, I slowly opened the door and raised my hands.

Emilio and I knew better than to fight as they whisked us into the waiting vehicles and sped through the city to the federal detention center for processing.

My head throbbed, and there was a whooshing sound in my ears with each pulse. My blood pressure had to be off the charts. I needed to calm down so I could think. I took a deep breath.

If I could make bail, I could run. Bail would be high, I was sure of that, but I could put up the house in Pennsylvania, and if that wasn't enough, I could beg and borrow from the family.

As soon as I was processed and allowed a phone call, I dialed Alexandra. She was going to be furious, but I knew I could trust her to do what I asked. She was my only hope of freedom.

"Hello?" Her voice sounded tired.

"Alexandra? Look . . . I'm incarcerated. I need you to get my attorney."

The words tasted like bile. I knew I didn't need to elaborate. She knew to call Schreiber.

"All right. . . . Do I need to know anything?"

That was it—no sweet words, no comforting assurances that I would beat this one. But with each word I heard an increasing sadness in her voice. I had failed her again.

"Just get me Schreiber. He'll take care of it."

"It's going to be harder to beat this time, Herman. Second-time offenders don't get the same breaks first-timers do."

Fear laced its icy fingers around my spine. I shivered, trying to shake free of it.

As a piece of architecture, the Metropolitan Detention Center in Brooklyn was uninspired, an abandoned warehouse with heavily armed guards.

I was escorted to a windowless unit called 5-North, home to 120 inmates.

"That's yours." The officer pointed to the top bunk. No one liked the top bunk, which is why it was assigned to newcomers.

My bunk creaked and groaned as I climbed onto it. The concrete ceiling, only a few feet from my face, had a musty smell. It was an achingly familiar view.

"Mendoza on a visit!" an officer shouted.

It had to be my attorney, because in MDC, family visits were called by the last digits of the registration number assigned to you at processing.

The corrections officer called me to the lawyer's visiting room, located adjacent to the general family visitation area. The man who sat across from me was not Mr. Schreiber.

"What's happened? Who are you?"

The man offered his hand. "I'm a colleague of Mr. Schreiber. He's asked me to take over your case as he sees to your brother's. I'm afraid Emilio's situation is much more complicated than yours."

"Of course."

"We have the affidavit in support of the application for arrest. It looks as if the investigation goes back nearly a decade and—"

"Ten years!" I almost choked at the words.

My lawyer nodded gravely and slid the affidavit across the table. I skimmed the first paragraph. *On or about and between January 1st, 1990, and June 28th, 1998, both dates being approximate and inclusive. . . .*

"It goes on to detail the involvement of several people within your organization, as well as the roles you and your brother played."

At the top of page one, in capital letters, was my name, listed alongside Emilio's and Dante's, even though he was already serving time upstate. I fumed when I got to the pages that confirmed John had been secretly recording our conversations. "That rat!"

He'd been wired the whole time. The report had details about a meeting we had with him by a gas station, where we handed him nine kilos of cocaine. He'd been handing us marked bills all along!

Emilio and I knew we were in deep. Now we knew that the investigation had been going on for a while. What we didn't know was that the DEA had drawn on all their resources to shut us down. The feds, the NYPD, and the New York City Tactical Narcotics Team had all worked together to collect information on us.

Despair washed over me. The evidence was overwhelming. I looked across the table at my attorney. There was no way that he or Schreiber could get us out of this one.

"So . . . what are we looking at for bail?"

29

ON THE RUN

Freedom could be mine for a cool half million.

I hated that I would have to put up the house in Pennsylvania as collateral, knowing that I intended to jump bail, but I promised myself I would get Alexandra something even better. That would only cover about half the bail money, though.

I couldn't ask my parents to help me out—they had already put their home up as collateral in order to get Emilio out on bail the first time. An image of Mami curled up on her bed in the fetal position, sobbing over Emilio's incarceration sprang to mind and made it hard to breathe.

I couldn't ask Alexandra's family to bail me out. I had never been in their good graces, and it made it worse when they found out about Daria's pregnancy.

My best option was my oldest brother, Gabriel. He hated that Dante, Emilio, and I had sold drugs, hated how much our activities hurt Mami. But he still loved us, and I was positive he would do everything he could to help.

———

I spent a month and a half in the concrete box that was the Metropolitan Detention Center. And after I posted bail, those first free breaths of polluted city air felt as fresh and welcome as any spring mountain breeze. It was exhilarating. And it made me hungry. I felt I could do with a hearty steak.

I pulled out my flip phone and looked through the short list of numbers. Rolando. He always enjoyed a satisfying meal.

"Hey, man. I'm out! Meet me at Tres Este?"

Tres Este was my favorite Italian restaurant. I ordered a drink and waved Rolando over when he came in.

Rolando gripped my hand in both of his. "You had us worried, man. I'm glad you're out."

I chuckled as if my release had been a guarantee. "How's business?"

He leaned in and shook his head. "It's slow, man. This case has everyone nervous. We're all watching our backs."

"Well, I'm back. We'll see what we can figure out."

When I met with my attorney later, he had bad news.

"It's likely the US district attorney will offer you a plea deal."

The words were meant to sound encouraging, but his face was grim.

"What do you think it'll be?"

"The prosecutor is asking fifteen years. It seems reasonable. US sentencing guidelines for the amount of cocaine trafficked and conspiracy to send more puts you at eighteen to twenty-five years."

He might as well have said life. The kids would practically be adults before I got out. I had managed to keep the business going the last few months, but that many years behind bars . . . there was no way I could come back from that.

I left my lawyer's office and headed straight for a nearby lounge. I climbed up on a bar stool and laid some cash on the counter.

"Give me a bottle of Rémy Martin."

I spent the next couple of hours draining that bottle and planning my escape. My life, once populated with people and parties, felt empty—a home of dark shadows.

My court date came and went. My lawyer must have waited hours for me to show. I liked the idea of wasting his time. He had, after all, wasted mine with his useless plea deal.

I was officially on the lam. I couldn't stay in any of my apartments or my home in Pennsylvania. Those would be the first places the feds would look.

I was concerned the cops would question my wife and pressure her into giving them information on my whereabouts. Out of precaution I had instructed Alexandra to communicate with me through public phones.

The feds probably expected me to hide in seedy underground haunts, but that wasn't me. If I stuck to upper middle-class areas, I could live comfortably and avoid suspicion. I called up my friend who owned a limo company.

"Hey, Pablo. I could use a ride. Can you pick me up?"

I gave him my location and ambled out to the curb. There seemed to be cops everywhere, but I'd learned that if you walked around with your head high, as if you hadn't a care in the world, they never even looked your way.

The limo pulled up to the curb in front of me a few minutes later, and I walked slowly and casually toward it. I climbed into the front passenger's seat.

"Herman! I didn't expect to hear from you. You're still free?"

"Yeah, and I'm tryin' to stay that way. Think you could put me up for a few days?"

"Of course, man. I got your back." He glanced over at me, and I caught a look of concern. "You'll be needing me to drive for you?"

I nodded. That was why I liked this guy—he could anticipate people's needs. It's what made him so successful in his business.

"Where do you want me to take you? I can take you back to my apartment if you want, but I won't be back for a while."

I didn't really want to be alone. "Can you drop me at the casino?"

It was familiar territory, but not so familiar that the cops would go looking for me there.

It was New Year's Eve, three months since I had skipped my hearing. A long time to be on the run.

"Hermano!" My friend Bill greeted me at the door of his apartment. "Come on in. Join the party!"

The "party" was just Bill and his girlfriend. He poured me a couple fingers of Jack Daniels; I drank it in one gulp.

"Here, have another."

Bill's speech was slurred, and his aim was off. He sloshed whiskey over the side of the glass and onto my hand. I shook it off and grabbed the bottle from him. He laughed, returning to the sofa and the waiting arms of his girlfriend.

We spent hours drinking and telling each other stories of stupid things we had done. Suddenly, Bill, emphasizing a point in his story, pulled out a 9-millimeter handgun, stumbled out to his balcony, and blasted two shots into the air.

The shots reverberated through the neighborhood. People screamed, and a few yelled for someone to call the police.

"Bill, you idiot!" I yelled.

His girlfriend ran from the apartment, not even stopping to put on shoes.

She was right to run. We all had to get out. I grabbed my jacket and slid into my loafers. As I ran from the apartment I spotted a patrol car searching behind the building. I cursed. Stupid Bill and his stupid 9-millimeter.

The officer's back was to me; Bill's car was only a hundred feet away. I jumped in and took off. It was a bad idea. I wasn't sober enough to drive.

I pulled over as soon as I was out of the area. It was a close call.

I abandoned Bill's car and walked back to Pablo's place. He wasn't home. My chest ached with loneliness. The start of a brand-new year was just hours away, and I was stuck alone at a friend's place. I had a wife. I had three children. I had multiple girlfriends. And I was alone.

I wondered what Alexandra and the kids would be up to. I hadn't seen them in so long—what if Adam had forgotten what I looked like? *Forget it! If I can't be with my family, I'll find the best party in town*, I decided.

Most of my friends were busy, but my cousin Frankie was around. I called him up and bought our way into the VIP section at the China Club, one of the hottest clubs in the Upper West Side. I ordered us a bottle of Cristal and danced my way through the crowd. Out of the corner of my eye I spotted a familiar face. I tapped Frankie's arm. "Hey, look. There's Marc Anthony."

"Where?"

"Over there. The booth in the corner."

Frankie wasn't a guy to sit back and watch things happen. My cousin went straight up to him and said, "Hey, Marc, what's up, man. My cousin, Herman, wants to meet you."

Frankie was a big guy with an even bigger personality, and no one denied his requests. He gave off the vibe that if anyone crossed him, he could, and would, knock them around the block.

Marc's bodyguard tensed, ready for a fight, but Marc motioned for him to sit down and walked over to meet me. "Hey, man, looks like you guys are a couple of big shots."

I laughed and poured him some Cristal.

He smiled and waved it away. "Estoy bien. I'm good." Then he pulled me into a quick hug. "Happy New Year!" Okay, so he was a pretty cool guy.

Frankie looked pleased with himself when he joined me again. "Now that you've got a story to tell, want to go? I want to hang out with my girl."

We'd only just gotten there, and it wasn't even midnight yet. But it wasn't going to be any fun if my cousin kept harassing me to leave, and no one denied Frankie's requests. I could always call up my barber, a good friend with some great connections. He was sure to have a line on some girls.

I was right.

We found ourselves at the coolest party in town, and for about ten minutes I forgot my woes. But as the hands on the clock ticked steadily toward midnight, images of Alexandra and countless New Years from the past played over and over in my mind. I missed her like crazy. What was I doing here? The kids were probably already in bed, dark curly hair dampened by sleep and splayed across their pillows.

I tipped back another glass of Cristal and moved on to a waiting glass of cognac. I had lost sight of my date and my friend, but I didn't care. Screw the consequences, I was going home.

I stumbled out of the club and found Pablo. "Take me . . . take me home."

He opened the car door for me and helped me in. He turned toward the apartment I had been staying in the last few days.

"No, no! Not there. Pennsylvania."

"That's a bad idea, man. You know you can't do that."

"Don-don't tell me what I can do. Am I paying you or not?"

30

THE TROPHY

I hadn't realized how tightly wound up I was until the lights of the city started to fade behind us. My muscles relaxed, and I sank deeper into my seat. Pablo was saying something, but his words were as much a jumble to me as the blur of the passing country-side. I had been drinking for almost twenty-four hours—maybe that was the reason for the strange feeling churning in my gut and running in shivers along my spine. I squeezed my forehead to ease the throbbing.

When we were only ten or fifteen minutes from my gated community in Pennsylvania, I started to get nervous. Maybe the feds expected me to go home for the holidays. They could be watching the main gate.

"Wait a minute. Slow down," I ordered. "Let's go in through the visitor entrance."

A limo on New Year's going through the guest entrance was no cause for alarm.

We pulled up to the gate, and I realized we had a problem; guests had to check in with the community's security officer before being allowed entrance.

Even wasted, I knew enough not to call Alexandra.

The security guard leaned out the window of the gatehouse. "You've come to visit? Or do you have a home here?"

"Yeah, I'm visiting family."

"What's the name and number?"

I felt a momentary panic. No one was expecting me. I wasn't sure if anyone was still awake. My sister-in-law had moved into the same community, but I was sure she would help me out. I gave the guard her number.

"And who should I say is visiting?"

"Jose," I said, giving her husband's name.

He dialed their number, and I hoped against hope that they'd let the fictional Jose in.

"Okay. Thank you. Happy New Year."

The guard hung up the phone, handed me a one-day pass, and waved us through.

As the limo pulled up to my home, my breath caught. It had always been a pretty spot, but now, soaked in the beauty of the winter night, it was overwhelming in its loveliness. Snow covered everything, shimmering like a million little diamonds in the light of the moon.

I looked over at Pablo, half expecting him to be as enraptured as I was. He wasn't even looking. His mouth was open in a wide yawn, and he was rubbing his eyes.

"Are you tired? You can sleep in our guest room."

He shook his head. "Nah, I'm just going to head back."

"Okay. Thanks, man. Drive safe."

With a wave, he got back in the limo and drove off as I stumbled up to the door and rang the bell.

I sometimes forgot how beautiful Alexandra was. She opened her arms to hug me, and I leaned into them. She pulled back almost immediately. "Herman, you stink. How much did you drink?" Disgust emanated in waves off of her.

It wasn't the welcome I'd hoped for, or even imagined. It had been a hard few months—couldn't she just bring me inside and hold me until all my fears and frustrations faded away?

Instead she watched as I staggered to the bedroom. I could barely make it to the bed, because my limbs refused to move according to my will. If I could just sleep off my drunken stupor, things would look better in the morning.

A high-pitched ringing invaded my subconscious. I pulled a pillow over my head and tried to block it out.

Alexandra picked up the phone.

"We have the DEA and State Police surrounding your house. Tell your husband to give himself up. Do you have any guns in the house?"

"None. . . . Nothing like that." Alexandra tucked the phone between her ear and shoulder and started to shake me.

"If you don't send Herman out, we will break your door down!"

Alexandra's voice sounded miles away, and the shaking irritated me.

"Don't you dare break my door down!" she commanded into the phone. "I have children in the house." She chucked the phone down and began shaking me with both hands.

"Herman, Herman . . . the cops have the house surrounded. It's over. Turn yourself in." The fear in her voice did more to wake me up than the shaking did.

Turn myself in? I couldn't do it. I wouldn't. I had been on the run for months. It was just a drunken moment of weakness that had brought me within their grasp.

I grabbed my pants from the end of the bed, pulled a T-shirt over my head, and slid into my sneakers. The room spun and I felt faint, but I stayed upright enough to stumble over to the bedroom window and throw it open. When half my body was out of the window I looked up, and I saw a police officer with his gun drawn.

"Police!" he screamed.

It was like a scene from a corny cop movie. But corny or not, it was obvious I wasn't getting past him. I pulled myself back inside. Alexandra stood watching me, her face a play of dread and apprehension.

"Open the door. It's over!"

They were on a megaphone now.

It felt as though the floor were falling away beneath me. There really was no way out. I followed Alexandra out of the bedroom, toward the entryway. She placed a hand on the doorknob. I wanted to ask her to wait, to give me a minute to prepare for the humiliation that was pressing in and would soon overwhelm me. But words refused to form in my dehydrated mouth.

Alexandra pulled open the door. "Put your guns down now! There are children in the house. He's coming out."

I walked toward the door, hands above my head. "I'm here," I croaked.

Behind me sounded a cry, then uncontrollable sobbing. I hadn't noticed until that moment that my sister-in-law Mary was visiting from Jackson Heights. I wanted to cry too. My whole body was vibrating with anxiety.

At the same time a dozen officers barged into our home, guns drawn. They brought me outside, and I realized I recognized a face in the crowd. It was the same DEA agent who had arrested me in New York all those months ago. He probably felt proud of himself, bringing me down after a long chase—a feather in his cap.

Outside the house it was a full-fledged frat party with people from all three agencies, federal, state, and local, laughing and patting each other on the back. Congratulating each other on a job well done.

As they handcuffed me, I begged for some water.

"Grab us a glass of water," the arresting agent called.

They must have had Alexandra get me one, because within minutes the officer was holding a glass of water to my mouth so I could drink. There was immediate relief, and it worked its way across the arid desert that was my tongue and cooled my scratchy throat. The relief went deeper than just the quenching of thirst. I wasn't running anymore. The worst had happened, and there was nothing to do but deal with it. It was over.

I glanced back up at the house, afraid of what I might see. I didn't see the kids—I couldn't even see Alexandra. The only people visible were a mass of DEA agents milling around, taking pictures. Trophy shots after a long hunt.

Signs for Scranton, Pennsylvania, home to the closest federal detention center, counted down the miles to my incarceration. I looked down at the black pavement whizzing by. If I could get the door open, I could jump out and kill myself. I could end it all right here.

"Officer?" The officer in the passenger's seat looked back at me.

"Can't you open the door? You know I'm never getting out of prison. It's over! I don't want to live." Tears welled in my eyes.

The officer looked at me with more pity than I deserved. "I'm not gonna lie—your case is big . . . but you never know what could happen."

There was kindness in his eyes and voice. Somehow, it comforted me. If he thought there was hope, maybe there was. I sat up and tried to regain some of the composure I had lost.

"Mendoza? Visitors!"

It had only been a few days, but Alexandra and the kids were allowed to visit during the week, and we didn't want to waste the opportunity.

"Daddy!" Adam pulled away from Alexandra, ran toward me, and banged on the bulletproof partition between us.

I sat down opposite them and placed my head against the glass. I could just make out the words "Daddy! I want to sit with you." The tears in his eyes tore at my heart. Alexandra picked up the heavy plastic phone, and I did the same. She placed her end against Adam's ear.

"Sorry, kiddo. I wish I could pick you up, but I can't."

"Daddy, please."

"Sorry, baby."

Alexandra took the phone back. "How are you doing? Are you all right?"

I shrugged. "I've been in worse places."

It wasn't the encouragement she was looking for.

The visiting area had a security system in place to monitor the visit. We talked briefly about the case and what to tell my attorney, but there was a lot I couldn't say.

Adam yanked the phone back from Alexandra's hand. "Daddy, just come play with us?"

"Sorry, buddy. I need to stay back here."

"But, Daddy, I can't touch you." He pressed his face against the glass. "Please, come play with me. Pleeease."

I sobbed into the phone. "I'm sorry, baby. I can't."

Sam grabbed the phone next, her voice equally confused.

"Can't you just come out for a little bit? Can't you tell them you'll be good?"

"Mendoza, time's up."

My allotted one hour had gone too quickly.

"Good-bye, baby."

There were tears in Alexandra's eyes too. We were all crying. Sam and Adam pressed their sweet little hands and faces up against the glass. I pressed my hand against the smooth surface, wishing they could feel the warmth of my touch.

"Mendoza?"

I nodded and stepped back, allowing the officer to escort me to a closed-off area where they again searched me for any concealed drugs or weapons, despite the fact that there was no possibility of any physical contact with my visitors.

Time passed slowly in my unit. My cellmate and I spent hours reminiscing about life on the outside. He was easy to talk to until one evening when he confided in me about his nightmares and totally freaked me out.

"I'm being tormented, man. It's like . . . it's demons or something. Definitely spiritual, but physical too."

The hairs raised on the back of my neck. I wanted to laugh it off like he was crazy, but I knew firsthand that there were some weird and unexplainable happenings in the world.

"It's like demons tell me what to do, and I guess I feel like I have to do it. Man, I know it sounds crazy, but it's real."

I'd never given much thought to angels and demons, but I couldn't deny his experience.

———

"They've set a court appearance for your extradition back to New York," my attorney said when he visited me a few days later. I could tell from his body language that he was not particularly pleased with me. "You'll have to face the charges for which you were initially apprehended."

I'd expected that, of course. And I was sure they had added a few more charges since then too.

Soon after I arrived at the courthouse for my appearance, my case was called.

"Do you want to waive the extradition or appeal it?" the judge asked in a bland voice.

"I waive it."

The judge made a quick note, then glanced up and nodded. "Then you will be sent back to New York to face charges."

31

Born Again

A guard locked shackles around my wrists. "Legs."

I spread my legs shoulder width apart, and they shackled my ankles and chained me to another inmate.

"Follow me."

It wasn't the first time I had participated in an awkward three-legged march to a federal secure transport. The transfer to New York meant my sentence was finally under way.

I knew where we were going as soon as we turned onto Third Avenue. Metropolitan Detention Center, Brooklyn. At least I knew what to expect there.

I attached my ID to my shirt, and they escorted me up to the fifth floor. Each floor was divided into two units: north and south. The last time I was here, I was assigned to 5-North. This time, I headed south.

I was the new guy again, which meant I was back on the top bunk. I really hated the top bunk, but by the time I got to my cell, I was too tired to be upset about it. I climbed up onto my new bed and drifted into unconsciousness.

Exhaustion still clung to me the next morning. My head ached, and my muscles felt weak. I couldn't bring myself to haul my body over the side of the bunk and fish around with my aching feet for the small ladder at the end just to eat an uninspired breakfast. I flipped onto my side, closing my eyes to the concrete wall in front of me.

I felt a tap on my shoulder. Softly, as if not to startle me, someone asked in Spanish, "Your name is Herman Mendoza?"

With a similarly quiet tone, I responded, "Yes. Sí, sí."

The man, another inmate from my housing unit, smiled and waved me down off my bunk. "Follow me. Your brother Emilio is in 5-North. He wants to see you."

A little zing like an electric shock went through my body. Emilio was here, in the same block! I hadn't talked to Emilio since he went to jail and I went on the run. I'd missed him.

I scrambled down and followed the man across the hall to the small recreational court. It didn't have any windows. It was just a gated space with a glimmer of light.

I spotted Emilio, who was looking even more excited than I was. He pulled me into a hug and then held me back to get a good look at my face. "Praise God!" he said with a grin.

An unusual exclamation for him. He shook his head in wonder. "God is so good. He answers prayers!"

I had no idea what he was talking about, but I could understand his enthusiasm. It's rare, in a federal criminal case, to have two co-defendants housed on the same floor, especially family members. It was kind of a miracle.

"Herman! I was praying God would bring you here so I could tell you about Him."

He prayed for me to be here? What is wrong with him, and why is he being so weird? I studied his face—it looked . . . different. There was a glow about him, a calm that I'd never seen before.

He caught me staring at him and grinned. "I'm different, huh?"

I shrugged, not sure how he wanted me to answer.

"I'm a new man, Herman. I've been born again. Saved!"

I'd heard the phrase before, but I didn't quite know what it meant. I laughed nervously. "Saved from what?"

He chuckled and patted my shoulder. "I'm glad you're okay, man. You're in 5-South?"

I nodded.

"Cool. I'm gonna pray you get transferred to my unit."

It was a weird reunion, not at all what I expected, but it gave me the sense that things would be all right.

———

"Mendoza, grab your things. You're being transferred."

I couldn't believe Emilio's prayer had worked!

I found him later in the rec area. "Did you hear? They moved me to your unit and let me join the cleaning crew so I could get a bottom bunk!"

He thumped my back in congratulations. "Praise God! That's awesome."

The more time I spent with Emilio, the more he seemed different. It was like a foreign person inhabited his body. Yes, there was still plenty of the old Emilio there, but there was something more. Peace. I had seen it in him that first day. It was still there, and somehow, if possible, it was even more evident.

A few days later, Emilio squatted down next to my bunk and rested an arm on the mattress, ready for a chat. "We have church services every day at the dayroom, if you want to come with me. I've been going for the past six months. God's changing my life."

The very fact that Emilio kept crediting God with the change in him was evidence that he really had changed. It was a curious development. I wanted what he had. "All right, I'll go."

"You will? Really?"

"Yeah, man. I'll come."

I had tried everything that was supposed to make me happy. I had more money and women than I could handle. I had nice cars. I went to all the best parties. I had a beautiful wife, three gorgeous kids, and a nice house in the Poconos. But I wasn't happy. It felt like I was grabbing at air—I could never grasp the thing I was really after. Maybe going to church would help me find that happiness I'd been chasing. It seemed to work for Emilio.

I followed my big brother through the rec area. A few inmates with headphones crowded around a couple of televisions, but otherwise there was very little going on out there.

At one end of the rec room was the quiet room. That's where the action was. A few dozen people crammed inside. Apart from the oddly happy inmates, the room had little to boast about. With bare walls and a few chairs, it looked bland and boring from the outside. But there was something beautiful in this room that couldn't be seen. It could only be felt.

Every day from seven to nine in the evening it filled up with men of all ages and descriptions. Emilio was one of them. He led me to a chair at the back, and I watched as the crowd of inmates sang and clapped rhythmically to a song I'd never heard before. Once the singing stopped, an inmate stood up at the front.

"Hello, I'm Leo Martes. It's a pleasure to welcome you here tonight." He said it again in Spanish before asking, "Do any of you have a testimony you would like to share?"

One of the other inmates shot up from his chair and started thanking God for healing him from a disorder he'd been suffering from. "And thank you for praying for my case. I had some really good news this week. Things are looking up."

This guy's story intrigued me. Had God really played a part in the outcome of his case?

Several other inmates shared their stories. How was it that so many of them credited God for their reduced sentence, or healing, or relationships? It was incredible.

Leo stepped forward once more and began to preach. I had never heard a priest or a preacher give a sermon like that. There was something really comforting in his words. The atmosphere in the room was totally different from the atmosphere just a few feet outside the door. Sitting there beside my big brother, listening to words of forgiveness, I felt myself relax.

"You blew it, Herman." I wouldn't say my lawyer's voice was angry exactly, but it held a steely resolve.

"Your actions sabotaged your case."

Okay, maybe he was angry.

"What? What do you mean?"

"I mean there is no way I can represent you after this."

"No. Noooo. I need you," I pleaded. "Please. Just keep on—"

"There is no trust anymore, Mr. Mendoza. Your running effectively ruined our attorney-client trust."

I couldn't speak. He was right. I didn't like it, but I understood. I exhaled slowly, caught a juddering breath, and did my best to apologize.

He held up a hand. "As I was trying to explain, our contract is legally binding. In order to dissolve it we will have to go before a judge. I have already secured a date for that hearing."

"Okay." The word came out slowly, the last syllable lingering. It wasn't okay, but there wasn't really anything I could do about it.

"Alexandra? I need to secure another attorney fast."

I hadn't had much contact with Alexandra since arriving at MDC, but I didn't know who else to call to take care of things outside for me.

"What do you mean? What happened to your attorney?"

"My old attorney and I dissolved our contract. There wasn't any trust anymore . . . but I found a new guy, and he thinks he can get my time shaved down to ten years. He's got a lot of experience with my type of case."

She sighed heavily. I could feel the weight of it through the receiver. "I guess he's your best bet. What do you need me to do?"

"We'll need to pay him the retainer. Fifteen thousand dollars."

I could practically hear her shaking her head. "We'll have to take out a second mortgage."

"I'm sorry, baby. I just don't know what else to do."

This miserable situation was of my own making. Despite bringing in ridiculous amounts of money for years, we were broke. I had blown too much money on fancy suits, gambling, and partying. Alexandra and the kids would be living below the poverty line. If

I could get my sentence shaved down, we would be together again and I could provide for them once more.

———

My new attorney sat across from me, biting his thin bottom lip. "I'll give it to you straight, Herman. The prosecutor's office wants to give you twenty-five years. I could try and get it down to ten years, but it isn't looking good."

I tried to preserve my composure, tried to steady my voice before I spoke. "How can this be happening?"

All the hope that had been building since retaining him was sucked out of me.

He shrugged a shoulder, his attitude much more nonchalant than I thought it should be. "There is not much I can do for you."

This guy, with all his hype and promises, has taken my money. And for what? Twenty-five years? No way. "Guard!"

The door opened behind me.

"I'm done here."

———

When I got back to 5-North, Emilio followed me to my cell.

"It's over, man. I'm never getting out." I flopped down on my bunk. "I won't get to see the kids again. . . . Alexandra will leave me. . . ." My words crumbled into racking sobs.

Emilio put an arm around my shoulder. "You never know. . . . Through Christ all things are possible."

I smiled a weak smile. I appreciated his encouragement. But why would God do anything for me? I was a waste. No, if things were going to get better, I'd have to handle them myself. I would fire my attorney and start again. I wouldn't just fire him—I would file a suit against him and recuperate our money!

———

"What do you mean, you lost the retainer?" I could hear Alexandra fuming on the other end of the line.

"He was a fraud. He lied to us. I had to fire him."

"Are you crazy? That was all we had. There isn't any money to get you another lawyer."

"Maybe we can—"

"No, Herman, no. 'We' aren't doing anything. I'm done. I don't want to see you or hear from you again. We're finished!"

I stumbled back as if she had punched me. I knew things were bad between us, but she had put up with everything else. *I need her. How can she just abandon me?* No. I wouldn't accept it. "Alexandra, baby, please. . . ."

The line went dead.

In my cell, I kicked at the wall until my toes ached. My case had hit rock bottom and so had I. I had a right to drown in misery, didn't I?

Fortunately, Emilio refused to let me wallow in self-pity. "Come to the service with me tonight. It'll get you out for a little while . . . and I think it's something you really need. God can help you through this."

I shrugged. I desperately needed help from something or someone. Why not God? There was an emotional and physical ache inside of me that wouldn't go away. Maybe Emilio's God could do something about that.

We approached the dayroom, and I started to feel jittery. Tonight, something felt different. Tonight, I had come looking for answers. Needing help. What if I didn't get it?

I sank down on a chair and looked around at the other inmates singing unfamiliar songs as if they were a practiced choir. Instead of joining them I let my mind drift back to all the things that had gone wrong in my life recently. It was an extensive list.

The singing ended, and Leo got up behind the makeshift pulpit. "Brothers, I want to talk to you tonight about the love of God. . . ."

As he preached the ache inside me began to shift.

"Psalm 139:18 tells us that his pleasurable thoughts about us outnumber the grains of sand! Can you imagine that?"

His words broke through the miserable fog in my brain and produced an unexpected sense of peace. It was strange, but good. Really good.

"And I'm not talking about a God who only loves us when we are doing what He wants us to. Romans 5 tells us that He loved us when we were still His enemies. Listen to Romans 5:8. 'God demonstrates his own love for us in this: While we were still sinners, Christ died for us.'

"I don't know what landed you in here. Maybe drugs, stealing, murder. I think it's pretty obvious that each and every one of us in this room is a sinner. Even if you never did what you were convicted of, I guarantee you've done things in your life that hurt others. Maybe it's an affair, or you took something from a brother that didn't belong to you. The truth is, we need a Savior. Someone to pull us out of the wretched hole we've dug for ourselves. Christ wants to meet you right where you're at. . . . "

It was as if the words he spoke were just for me. I couldn't help but reflect on all the things I had done or experienced in my life and where they had led me: prison . . . literally and figuratively. *Even if I escape from this place, I can never escape the prison of my past.*

Just as that thought formed in my mind, Leo said, "God has a way out for you."

His words rocked me.

"He can give you peace in the midst of what you are going through."

Could He?

Things were getting weird. It seemed as if he were reading my mind.

But, I told myself, *his words are still general enough that they could apply to most of the men here.*

Leo went on, "There is someone here tonight who is thinking about his past. Longing for a way out. Wondering if life is worth living."

My heart pounded hard in my chest. *Did God tell him to say that?*

"God wants you to know He can fill that void. He can carry you through. You will still have to face the consequences of your sins, but Christ will change the way you experience your circumstances."

The same peace I had sensed the first time I attended the service settled over me again.

"Christ can make you a new person. You can be born again."

The fog cleared from my mind. I finally realized what it meant to be born again, and I believed it!

"Today God's calling you to enter into His rest, and I assure you, your life will be filled with His presence. I want to invite you to come and pray with us now."

I jumped out of my seat and hurried down the aisle to the front of the room. I fell to my knees, sobbing.

The weight of my sins and their far-reaching consequences hit me. Flashing through my mind were acts of sin against God and things I'd done that hurt others. Just moments before, if I had thought about my wrongdoings, I would have attempted to justify them. But now I thought about all the people who might have killed or been killed as a result of the drugs I had sold. I thought about the women who may have sold their bodies in order to feed their habits and mothers who were heartbroken about drug-addicted children. I was convicted about the way had I treated my wife, how unfaithful I was to her. I needed Alexandra more than ever and felt that I had never been there for her and my family. My three children were innocent victims of all my lies and deception. I felt for my parents and all of the years of pain I caused them, and for all the women I had lied to and manipulated in exchange for my personal pleasures.

In that moment, I saw clearly that I was a sinner. People talk about life flashing before your eyes when you die—maybe that's what was happening to me. The old Herman was being put to death, and I was becoming a new person in Christ, just like Emilio had talked about.

There at the front of the little quiet room in Metropolitan Detention Center, I cried out, "Forgive me! God, forgive me! I'm sorry.

I've been so wrong. Please, God, forgive me." As the words tumbled out I was overcome by the strangest feeling. A warmth enveloped me, and it felt as though some dark evil were literally being ripped out of me. God took it.

All that guilt and shame, all the dark deeds . . . it felt as if He had physically reached inside me, taken them out, and filled that space with light. It was overwhelming. Incredible. Never had I even heard of God doing something like that, but He had just done it for me! I continued to cry, but they were tears of relief and gratitude.

People talk about a spiritual awakening, but that term seems too weak to describe what happened to me. It wasn't just waking up—the world suddenly looked different to me now. It was like wearing glasses for the first time and discovering that you can see leaves on the trees and not just an amorphous blob of color.

That evening after the service, Emilio found me, a wide grin plastered on his face. It almost rivaled my own.

"I was praying for you, Herman. Praying day and night for your salvation. This is a huge answer to my prayers! You have no idea how worried I was about you. I was scared you'd be killed out there. I asked God to spare you and send you here so that I could tell you about Him. And He heard me! You're saved!"

I could see him fighting happy tears. His was a peculiar prayer, when I thought about it—asking God to send his brother to prison. But it was the right prayer to pray. For me, there would have been no other way.

My transformation produced some interesting side effects. I suddenly had a desire to make amends to all the women I had lied to and used. That meant making some difficult phone calls. Alexandra still refused to talk to me, but there were other women I had hurt. I started calling them one by one.

"Heather? I just wanted to call and tell you that I'm a Christian now, and I'm sorry for using you. I'm married to a wonderful woman, who I love very much. Please, forgive me for misleading you."

"What are you talking about? You got religion?"

I grinned. "I guess you could say that."

She gave a snort of derision. "You're kidding, right?"

"No, I'm serious, and I just wanted you to know—"

"Forget it." She laughed again. "You've lost it, haven't you? You've gone crazy in there." She hung up before I could contradict her.

Next I tried Mami. Apart from Alexandra, she was the person I had hurt the most. For nearly two decades I had deceived and used her. I had made her worry and played her for a fool—and despite it all she had loved me.

"Mami? It's me. I just wanted to tell you what happened to me."

As we talked, I asked for her forgiveness and told her how God had made me a whole new man.

"That's really . . . nice . . . Herman."

I had spoken with passion and sincerity, and she was happy to hear my story, but I had a track record. The wounds were deep. I had lied to her so many times before, and it would take time for her to believe me.

I had never realized the Bible was such a cool book. I had no interest in reading it before, but now I couldn't get enough of it. Every time I opened it I learned something. Stories like those of David and Goliath or Noah's ark, which had once seemed juvenile, came alive. Each one suddenly seemed extremely important.

I flipped through the book of Psalms, which were really songs and poems. Many of them were written by King David, a shepherd boy turned king of Israel. By all appearances, our lives couldn't be more different. Yet there was so much I could relate to. The Psalms weren't just poetry, but a record of the inner spiritual life of this man who knew and loved God.

The New Testament stories of Jesus carried a gravity and profound meaning that I hadn't noticed before. The more I studied and learned about the love of God, the more it began to work in me. I was in awe of the power of forgiveness. I wanted to talk about it with anyone who would listen.

I flipped to the gospel of Mark, and my eyes rested on the words "For what shall it profit a man, if he shall gain the whole world, and lose his own soul?" (Mark 8:36 KJV).

I felt sick to my stomach. That was me! I had thought I was living in freedom before, but looking back, I realized I was depressed and lonely. I had to drink myself into a stupor just to get through the day. For years I had walked the road of destruction. I could have lost my soul!

Suddenly, it didn't even matter anymore that I was behind bars; I was freer here than I had ever been. I wanted to shout from the rooftops that the power of God is incredible and that when you give your life to Jesus, you'll see Him at work all over the place. This was more life-giving and exhilarating than anything else I had tried before.

32

5-North

"You know, Emilio. I've been thinking."

My older brother looked me over and chuckled. "If you'd said those words a few months ago, I would have assumed you had some scheme to break out of jail or to run the business from the inside. But you're different now."

He was right. It was pretty amazing how much I had changed in so short a time.

"So, shoot. What have you been thinking about?"

"I was thinking that God has a reason for us to be here together, and incarceration's not gonna deter me from the purpose God has for me."

Emilio slapped my arm. "Exactly, bro! I think God wants to use us here too. We just gotta get ready."

———

Leo was leaving. He had already served five years of his seven-year term at MDC while waiting for the outcome of his case. He would likely move soon to complete whatever time he had left elsewhere.

It was hard to imagine what we were going to do without our jailhouse pastor. It felt a little like he was abandoning us, even though it wasn't his choice at all.

"I don't want to leave without having someone to take my place." He looked at Emilio and nodded thoughtfully. "Would you lead this church?"

Leading was a very different thing from attending and supporting.

"Yes. Okay." Emilio's voice held resolve even if his body language showed doubt. He turned to me. "Would you be my assistant? I could use a copastor."

I agreed. I really wanted to serve more. I wanted to share about the incredible things I was learning from the Bible every chance I could. In fact, this might be the very thing we felt God was preparing us for, but like Emilio, I was still so new in my faith. I had so much to learn.

"Do you think we can get some training?" I asked Emilio when Leo had left. "Maybe we should write to someone and ask for help."

"Yes, definitely. Let's send out some letters. See what kind of help is out there."

I got us some paper and pens, and we got right to work on letters to various Christian institutions: Gideons International, American Bible Society, and local churches.

"Make sure you're clear on what we're looking for," Emilio reminded me. "We don't wanna waste their time."

I was becoming a pretty good letter writer. Not only did I write to an enormous number of organizations, but I started writing to Alexandra. I sent her Bible verses along with my apologies. I knew she might not read them, but I hoped and prayed she wouldn't throw them out. Almost every time I spoke with Mami, I asked her to pass on a message to Alexandra. But no matter what Mami said, Alexandra would brush it off. She didn't even want to hear my name.

"Package for Mendoza. Herman Mendoza."

Glee bubbled inside me. The Christian groups Emilio and I had written to had come through for us. Almost every day for a week there had been a package for "Mendoza." Between the two of us, we had received dozens of Bibles and basic Bible courses.

I ripped open the brown-paper packaging and found a small stack of books. I flipped through the pages. I had only read a few lines and already felt like I was learning something new. It was like Christmas had come early.

I sat down with Emilio later that afternoon as he prepared for the evening service. "You know what's weird? The more I study, the more I realize how little I know."

"Yes! Exactly. I get that." Emilio closed his Bible on his fingers, keeping his place. "It's like . . . there are some things that are simple truths, easy to understand. You believe it or you don't, but if you do, it will change your life. But then, once you believe, it's like God just keeps showing you more and more about His character, and you realize He isn't simple. He isn't one-dimensional. He's so complex."

"It's like an infinite well. You can drop a bucket in and pull up fresh water from the surface, but that well goes deeper than you can measure."

I loved these talks with Emilio. I came away from them feeling excited. And there was a feeling I realized I had never really experienced before: joy.

There had been times in my life when I had been really happy, and most of those involved Alexandra and the kids. But that happiness was always based on my circumstances. Now I was in the very place I had made every effort to avoid. My circumstances seemed grim, but I felt a joy inside of me that I couldn't explain.

Inmates started to trickle in and find places in the small room. I spotted a new face, but a familiar one, among the crowd at the back of the room.

"Jayson?" I made my way to the back. It was him. My old friend from the neighborhood. "Jayson!" I called again.

I was right beside him before he figured out where my voice was coming from. "Herman? You're here too?"

"Yeah, man. I've been here awhile." I pulled him into a hug.

The last time I had seen him was in a hospital in Queens. He had been shot eight times outside of Las Brisas before falling through the glass. It was a miracle he'd survived. We must have been about nineteen at the time. Alexandra and I were newly married, and she came with me to visit him.

"Let's catch up after the service?"

Jayson nodded, a strange look on his face.

When the service was over, a few other guys and I helped tidy the chairs and stack books. Jayson had left before it was even over, but he couldn't have gone far.

I found him watching TV in the rec room. When he saw me, he got up and followed me to a table.

"I still can't believe you're here, man." I grinned as he sat across from me.

"I just finished doing state time, but I still have federal time to finish up, so they transferred me here."

"Crazy."

He shrugged. "Yeah. They picked me up for some homicide I had no part in. But they needed to pin it on someone."

The whole time he talked, his eyes studied my face. It was like he was sizing me up.

"You look different, man. I guess you'll tell me it's 'cause you got religion, but I mean . . . even your eyes look different."

I laughed. I couldn't help it. I felt different, but I hadn't realized the change was physical too. "I am changed, Jayson. I can't even tell you how good it feels to know Jesus. I feel free, and I have this joy. . . . I can't even describe it."

His eyes searched my face. "Really?"

I nodded.

"Crazy."

33

PASTORS IN CHAINS

"This is Reverend Leroy Ricksy from the Church of the Resurrection in East Harlem. Tonight I want to share a little story of something Jesus did right here in our church. . . ." The man's voice was dulcet and mellow, radiating comfort. Every Friday, Emilio and I tuned in to listen to his sermons, and his messages resonated in our very hearts.

His church was around the same size as ours here in 5-North, and it sounded like the members of his church and community struggled with the same issues many of us did: loneliness, addiction, temptation.

Leroy's church may have only numbered eighty people, but his radio ministry had more than a thousand supporters and many more faithful listeners. It was inspirational.

By the end of the program that night, I was in tears. Much like me, Reverend Ricksy had been through a huge transformation. He went from a drunk and a hobo to a man of God with multiple degrees and a growing ministry.

"God," I prayed, "please teach me and lead me, the way you have this remarkable man."

"You know what I wish we had?" Emilio asked me a few days later.

"What?"

"A spiritual mentor. Someone nearby who would write to us and pray for us and hold us accountable. It's too bad we don't have any contacts like that."

I nodded thoughtfully.

Emilio continued, "What about Reverend Ricksy?"

"He doesn't know us, but he's a Christian brother. We could at least ask. He doesn't know it yet, but he's already taught us a lot. We could see if he wants to make it official," I said.

I tried to tamp down my hope, but the thought that Reverend Ricksy would even consider being our mentor sent a shiver of excitement through me. "So . . . should we ask him?"

In response, Emilio pulled out some paper and started writing.

That Friday when we tuned in to Reverend Ricksy's program, we got our answer.

"I want to start our program tonight with a letter I received this week from some men who came to faith in Jesus while in prison."

I drummed on Emilio's arm. "That's us! He's reading our letter."

"This prison church in MDC 5-North has more members than my congregation. We need to respond. I am happy to become their mentor, but as their church family, let's encourage our brothers in Brooklyn."

His mellifluous voice was music to my ears. I couldn't stay seated. Emilio couldn't either. We slapped each other on the back and stomped around in circles, laughing and grinning like crazy people. "Thank you, Jesus!" we shouted in unison.

Our first letter from Reverend Leroy Ricksy came just a day later—the start of a long-term mentorship.

Soon after, another letter came from a woman by the name of Betty General. She explained that she was one of Reverend Ricksy's longtime listeners and supporters. She signed her letter *Momma B*, and it was full of such love and warmth that it was impossible not to feel instant affection for her.

We wrote right back to Momma B, thanking her for her prayers and support and telling her a little about what we felt God had called us to.

Her next letter came with a small donation. "It's not much, but please use it to get anything you might need to help run your ministry."

I flopped down in an empty chair beside Emilio, my heart full. "God is awesome, isn't He?" I had never felt this way on the outside. I had never been as excited about our business as I was now about our little chapel in 5-North.

Emilio took a good look at me and chuckled. I had a feeling I looked a lot like a teenage boy, starry-eyed over his first love. The truth was, I was starting to discover what real love looks like.

People who had never met us, who knew our history and our current residence, were writing to support and encourage us. Why? Because God had prompted them to. In a million different ways, God was showing us that He loved us. He was growing our confidence, knowledge, and ability, and because of that the prison ministry was gaining momentum.

Emilio suddenly got up from his chair and started to pace. "You know, if things keep growing the way they are, we'll need a bigger space to meet."

"We'll have to pray about that. I don't think the warden's comfortable with such a big group of prisoners holding meetings every day."

I was right about the warden. A short time later, he started an investigation. He refused to believe that so many inmates voluntarily attended church. Rumor had it he thought Emilio and I were organizing a riot.

He could investigate all he wanted, but there were no planned riots, no escape plots; all he would discover was that the Mendoza brothers wanted everyone in their unit to know Jesus.

"Have you met the new guy yet?" asked Julio, one of our regular chapel members.

"Not yet," I said. "When did he get here?"

"This morning. An Asian guy."

"You want to go tell Emilio? I'll get a welcome pack and meet you in the dayroom."

You never knew who you were going to encounter when a new guy came. He could be really hostile, really timid, or anywhere in between. Pretty much everyone came with a lot of baggage—fear, depression, anxiety, loneliness. Our 5-North church wanted to make sure they felt loved and welcomed right from the start.

We found the new guy just outside his cell. He looked a little nervous as we approached him. I held out the welcome pack. "Welcome to unit 5-North. Here's a Bible, slippers, and some food—welcome to the house of God."

His stubby eyebrows shot up, the typical reaction.

"It's not much," Emilio said. "Just some sandals and snacks. We just want you to know we're happy to help you settle in."

We introduced ourselves.

"I'm Christopher." As he inspected the welcome pack, his expression shifted from wariness to hope. "Thanks for this."

"Our pleasure, man." Julio slapped him on the shoulder. "We also wanted to invite you to our chapel services every evening. You might want to come early, because you won't get a seat otherwise."

Christopher's face lit up. "No kidding? Man, that's awesome. Yeah, I'll come."

True to his word, Christopher Yuan wandered into the dayroom a good fifteen minutes before anyone else. It gave Emilio and me a chance to get to know him better.

"I have to admit, I was a little surprised that you were so eager to come. We usually have to ask several times before a new guy decides to check out our services," I said, sitting down in the chair behind his.

He turned to face me, and I noticed again the light in his eyes. His next words confirmed my suspicions. "No way—I was excited to hear about this. I'm a Christian too."

People started filtering in, and the volume in the room made it difficult to hold a conversation, but I was curious to know how this Christian brother ended up serving time. It was at a group sharing time a few days later that Christopher opened up about his conversion.

"Hi. I'm Christopher Yuan," he said and waved. A brief, encouraging round of applause sounded in response.

"I guess you could say that God was calling me for years. He protected me even when I was rebelling and running from Him. I won't go into all the details, but I got heavily into drugs for a while. I flunked out of dental school and started dealing. My life was in this death spiral.

"Fortunately, I got caught. A dozen federal drug enforcement agents knocked on my door and found the equivalent of nine tons of marijuana." He gave a little chuckle at the memory.

"My arrest was the best thing that could have happened to me. I got a little Gideon Bible just before I was sentenced and started reading it. Then on the bunk above my own, I saw someone had written, 'If you're bored, read Jeremiah 29:11.' It said that God had good plans for us, to give us hope and a future. I wanted that. I'd heard some bad news about my health, and it seemed like a death sentence. It was like God was telling me to surrender to Him. He still had plans for me. The moment I surrendered, He changed me. I had been struggling with my own demons for so many years. I hated who I was. I hated who my parents wanted me to be. I felt like I would never belong anywhere, that I could never be loved. But God changed that. I feel freer now than I ever have. I am more myself, because I am looking to Christ for my identity." *

The round of applause when he finished was loud and long. His story may have had different details, but the struggles and hurts and eventual freedom he found within prison walls were things many of us shared.

Out of a Far Country by Christopher Yuan and Angela Yuan (Waterbrook, 2011) shares more of Christopher's amazing journey.

34

ALL IN

"We . . . gotta . . . do . . . something!" I was out of breath when I found Emilio.

He must have noticed how shaken I was; my whole body felt like it was vibrating. "Did you see what happened?" Concern choked his voice. I barely managed a nod.

Alarms had been ringing for who knew how long. Prisoners were hurried back to their bunks, and doors were locked.

"I was just in the rec area counseling someone. . . ." I shivered, remembering. My lungs burned, and I was borderline hyperventilating. "Suddenly, I felt this evil presence, and I looked over, and there was this guy standing there. He pulled out this thing, kind of like an ice pick, and he just . . . he just attacked this other guy. It was savage!"

"So that was the reason for the lockdown. . . ."

I nodded. "Something's got to change. We need to pray against this."

Emilio agreed. "We should start a prayer chain. We can get our guys to join. Just think what could change around here if we did that."

I let out a long breath of relief, slowly calming down.

A lot had happened for Emilio and me in a year. We'd been baptized along with many others from our 5-North church. We'd started long-distance seminary courses. We'd launched a prayer chain. And God was changing lives. You could feel an atmosphere of peace around 5-North. The norm was frequent fights, stabbings, and constant lockdowns. But the violence in our units had decreased rapidly, and the shakedowns were down to a minimum.

God was still broadening our vision. Our cases were still pending, and we had no court dates set, but we were so into our prison ministry that our current legal issues didn't seem to matter.

Together, Emilio and I went to pick up supplies for the welcome packs we gave to new inmates—we had assigned some of the church members to store the supplies in their lockers.

"Have you ever heard of something called an evangelistic crusade?" he asked.

"Like those big stadium events with Billy Graham where he speaks and hundreds of people give their lives to God?"

He snapped his fingers. "Exactly! I think we should do one of those. We don't just have a responsibility to our little church. We have life-saving information, and it needs to be shared."

I smiled. Our little meeting room was already getting crowded. It was a good problem to have, but we could only imagine what would happen if even more men in our unit became Christians.

"The thing is," I pointed out, "there's still so many guys that just don't want to come to the services. But if we could just get their attention and give them a reason to come . . . if we brought the service to them . . ."

Emilio rubbed a hand across the back of his neck. "We'll need to ask the unit counselor if we can use the rec room. It's not something they normally like to do."

———

"Yeah, I can't see any problem with it," the counselor said when we asked.

"We'd like to save up food and do a special supper. Would that be okay? Can we get permission?" I asked.

He laughed. "You guys. You want me bending the rules till they break."

We grinned sheepishly.

"Yeah, fine. Go ahead. Do what you can."

Emilio rolled out the plan to our church members. "And we can use the microwaves in each dormitory to cook for everyone. Sound good?"

There were questions, of course. "So, you're saying a hundred people might come, and we are going to feed them all?"

"Jesus fed over five thousand people with five loaves of bread and two fish. I think He can help us feed 5-North. We just need some cooks."

Over the next few weeks our guys brought offerings of little packs of mackerel and tuna from the commissary. Emilio asked a few guys with cooking skills if they would help, and they readily agreed.

Free food proved a good enticement. Dominican-style rice and fish may not seem that exciting, but it was a change from our usual fare, and the guys who prepared it were incredible cooks. Over a hundred men came through the food line.

The evangelistic crusade had the exact impact we'd hoped it would. After the men's bellies were full, we invited them to stay for the service, and most did.

I stepped into the area we had marked as a stage and looked out at the sea of faces packed into the rec area. I had volunteered to lead some singing. *What was I thinking?*

I cleared my throat and did my best to hit the first note. We'd chosen songs our church was familiar with, and they joined in right away. The rec area had better acoustics than the quiet room. Deep baritones boomed out, mixing with tenors and a few basses. It wasn't perfect. But it was beautiful to see hearts turning to God in worship.

Emilio's message that night was powerful. At the end, he looked around the room, meeting the eyes of so many men who had been broken before they had even been locked away. "Maybe you are ready to turn your back on your old life. Maybe you are ready to accept the peace and freedom that Jesus offers. If any of you want to pray with one of us, why don't you come on over? We're gonna pray and invite God to be a part of your lives."

My heart ached with gratitude as one by one, men from all areas of the room moved toward the front for prayer. We were going to need a bigger church space.

35

Alexandra Pays a Visit

Alexandra had been serious when she told me she was done with me and she was done with trying to hold it all together. She figured that if I could spend most of our married life acting irresponsibly—partying, drinking, and cheating—she could take a little time away from responsibility too.

What Alexandra didn't know was how much I was praying for her.

That same week, Mario, one of my fellow inmates, tracked me down. "Hermano, I have an idea. I was thinking of the prayer request you shared in the service last night—and I have a court appearance coming up. They'll decide if I'll be deported or sentenced to five years in prison." He looked like he was waiting for me to figure out what his idea was, but I had no clue.

"If I pray and fast for the salvation of your wife and for your case, will you pray and fast for me?"

"Great idea!"

Sometimes it is easier to have faith that your prayer for someone else will be answered than it is to have faith for your own situation.

"Let's commit to only water for three days and be in prayer for each other's needs," Mario said.

Not eating for three days really does help you remember to pray. On the fourth day, I practically ran to Mario's cell. When I got there, I found an officer tidying it up.

"What's going on?" I asked.

He pushed a broom across the floor as he answered, "He went home. He was released by deportation."

I whooped, almost making him drop his broom. It was exactly what we had hoped and prayed for. Without a doubt, it was a miracle.

Thank you, Jesus! I prayed as I walked back to my own cell.

The question now was, Would God answer Mario's prayer for me?

Two days later, I was called down to the visiting area. At first I thought it might be Mami or Papi. But something in my spirit must have known the truth. My hands were clammy, and I was sweating when the officer escorted me into the visiting area.

On the other side of the room sat my wife.

I was ecstatic. She was really there! God was so good.

My beautiful Alexandra was right in front of me—and she looked ticked.

Before she had a chance to get down to business, I needed to tell her what an answer to prayer her visit was, but I was smiling so big it was hard to speak. "Alexandra, baby. It's so good to see you."

She frowned.

"Herman, I have something I need to tell you." She inhaled deeply. "I came here to—"

I couldn't let her say it. I needed to apologize first. If I didn't, she might say her piece and run away. "Alexandra, baby, I have something to share with you too! It's about your future. Your destiny. This could change the course of your life."

She wasn't pleased that I'd interrupted.

I rushed on, "First, I want to ask you for your forgiveness. I've been a bad husband, a bad father. I've been unfaithful . . . and a menace to society."

Alexandra's look of steely resolve suddenly softened.

"I want you to know the same loving God who saved me. He turned my life around with His love, grace, and mercy. Alexandra, you can experience that too."

I had rehearsed the words a thousand times in my head. Played out her possible responses a million times. But her reaction still surprised me.

She began to cry. Her cries turned to sobs. It was hard to watch her, but I knew that this was a much better reaction than the cold, deaf ear I had expected. The Holy Spirit was working in her.

As she cried I felt pressed to carry on. I needed to share everything on my heart and let God take care of the details. I told her that even if she never came back to me, all I wanted was for her to be saved. "Alexandra, no matter what you've done, God can change your sadness to joy. He can take your sins away and make you whole, just like He did for me."

When she could speak, she told me about the last twelve months. "I've been partying . . . drinking way too much. And . . . and I've been unfaithful too." The words came out between shuddering breaths, but as she confessed, I could see God working, building in her a new heart.

Alexandra's eyes met mine. "I want Jesus in my life. I want to have the same peace and love I see in you. I want the God that forgave you to save me too. I want Jesus."

They were the sweetest, most beautiful three words I'd ever heard. More emotional and profound than even our wedding vows.

Through happy tears, I led her in prayer. "Father, I know I'm a sinner, and I ask for your forgiveness. I believe you died for my sins and rose from the dead. I want to turn from my sins, and I invite you to come into my heart and life. I want to trust and follow you as my Lord and Savior. In Jesus' name I pray. Amen."

We looked at each other and smiled.

"You know . . . I came to talk to you about a divorce," she confessed. "I thought I didn't love you anymore. But I think God really did do something. Because I do love you . . . very much."

I wiped at the tears that hung from the bottom of my chin. It was too wonderful to believe. "I love you, Alexandra. God is so good!" I laughed as more tears dripped down my cheeks. "I've been praying and praying for you. And now—it's a miracle, isn't it?"

Alexandra nodded. "I still can't believe it. I almost don't know what to do next. I just know I'm not going home as the same person."

We talked about the kids and what it would mean for them. We talked about my case, and we agreed to pray and trust the Lord in whatever He had planned for me. I told her about my baptism and how I wished she had been there.

"You should do it too, Alexandra. Find a church as soon as you can and get baptized."

"Time's up!" a guard called from the door.

It was too soon. We still had so much to share, so much to catch up on.

"Call Emilio's wife!" I suggested as I got up to head back to my cell. "She gave her life to the Lord a little while ago. You'll have a lot to talk about."

"I will. Thank you, Herman. I love you."

———

When Alexandra left MDC, she headed straight for my sister-in-law Veronica's place. She told me later how they had talked late into the night about how God had transformed their husbands.

When they couldn't keep their eyes open anymore, they said their good-nights.

"Don't forget to set your alarm," Veronica said. "I'll take you to church in the morning!"

As they pulled into the parking lot the next morning, Alexandra laughed. "This is the church? I used to go to school around here."

They walked through the doors, and Alexandra did a double take. "This hallway feels so familiar."

It was confirmation that it was where Alexandra was meant to be. It was a place she already felt comfortable in.

After the sermon they talked to the pastor.

"I'm really new to this," Alexandra confessed, "but I'd really like to be baptized."

He smiled. "Awesome. How about Tuesday?"

When Alexandra returned for her baptism on Tuesday, she was struck again by how familiar the building was. She racked her brain for a minute, trying to remember when she might have been to this church before.

"Ha! No way," she told Veronica. "This is where I used to party at, back in high school." She shook her head in amazement. "It seems like an eternity ago."

She told me how she put a white gown on over her clothes and stepped into the water of the baptismal tank. The pastor stood with her, one hand on her back and one holding her wrists, and said, "You may not understand everything that is going on in your life right now, but God is going to raise you up as a new creation."

Alexandra was taken aback. She had told him very little about her situation, but he was right. Then he whispered, "In good season, you are going to understand perfectly well."

He leaned her back into the water. It enveloped her for just a moment before he pulled her back up. Alexandra came out of the tank refreshed. All the garbage from the past washed away, and in its place was a peace she'd never felt before.

———

Alexandra's letter came the next week. Not only was she taking my calls, but she was writing and sending pictures from the kids as well.

Please pray that I can find a church here in Pennsylvania. I don't even know where to start.

It took almost no time at all for God to answer that prayer. In her next letter she told the story of the incredible way God provided.

I tried out a place called Shawnee Tabernacle in Tobyhanna. I think the kids and I will really love it there. Pastor Bloom and his wife are great. When I told Mrs. Bloom I was a brand-new believer, she drew me aside and said, "Sometimes in the church you'll find wolves in sheep's clothes, but don't allow that to deter you from coming to church."

At first it sounded like a warning, but it was just what I needed to hear. It's true—some people come to church claiming to be Christians, but they don't know Jesus. They are wolves in sheep's clothing who have their own agenda. But that should not keep us from attending church and showing the true love of God to others.

It was such a relief to know that Alexandra had not only found a church, but that the people were so welcoming and supportive.

Her letters continued to be filled with news about the Blooms. Pastor Dennis offered her a job as a pre-K teacher at the church. Samantha and Adam started attending the Christian school there, which meant Alexandra could take them to work with her in the morning. Alexandra was living far away from church in a new apartment, and when Pastor Bloom realized that she was struggling with her commute, he offered that she and the kids could move into the first floor apartment in their house. It was just what my family needed. Our heavenly Father was taking care of us.

36

Moving On

I could tell Philip Nabel was vastly different from my previous lawyer. He was sure of himself, but without the smug arrogance some top attorneys carried.

"I'm not going to make you any promises about the outcome," he said, sitting across the table from me, "but I do promise I will fight for you."

This was the second answer to Mario's fasting and prayers!

"To be honest, Mr. Nabel, that's all I want. I am trusting God for the outcome, but I still want a lawyer who will do their best to plead my case. I couldn't have said that to you eighteen months or so ago, but I gave my life over to Jesus, and whether I serve Him inside or outside, I know that I have a purpose now."

There was doubt in his eyes as he listened. I'm sure he thought I was throwing around the name of Jesus and talking about being born again in order to get a reduced sentence. His skepticism wasn't unfounded—there are inmates who do that with their lawyers. But in time, Mr. Nabel would see the truth.

It was a few months after the terrible events of 9/11 that my sentencing date arrived.

There had been a lot of prayer leading up to this day between Alexandra, Emilio, and some of the guys from 5-North church. Even though I tossed and turned most of the night, my mind running through all possible scenarios, I still felt like God was going to do something amazing.

There was the chance that the majority of my life and ministry would be in prison. If that was God's will, He would keep me and bless me through it, but I really couldn't believe that it was. Didn't the Bible say that He came to set the captive free? I knew that meant that we are captive to sin, but I just sensed that God was going to be literal in this.

It was after one in the morning when I finally fell asleep. Fewer than four hours later, a federal officer came to my cell and woke me up. "Time to go, Mendoza. You're in court this morning."

I sprang up, tired but fully conscious. I climbed out of my bunk and quietly knelt beside it, trying not to wake my cellmate. "Lord, have your way. Be glorified in all that will take place today. I trust in you no matter the outcome. But Lord . . . if it's your will, please give me a shorter sentence so I can be with my family again. Please, God, bless this day and this hearing. In Jesus' name, amen."

The holding cell at the federal courthouse was surprisingly clean. This seemed to be one of the differences between federal and state.

I waited—praying, pacing, and trying not to let my nerves get the best of me. It was about nine o'clock when my attorney came and federal court officers escorted me to a partitioned room where we could speak.

Mr. Nabel looked at me curiously before starting. "Herman, I have bad news. I've been looking at your probation report. They've done a full report on your criminal activity, your family ties, and your parole violations. The Probation Department is recommending the sentence of a minimum of one hundred eight months up to one hundred thirty-five months of incarceration."

The news hit me like a punch in the gut. I had been so sure. . . .

"But I think we can do better. I will try to get you much less than that, but I want you to be prepared."

I had waited nearly four years for this hearing. I didn't want to prepare for the worst. I wanted to have hope. I wanted to trust God for a miracle, but it was hard to fight despair.

God's in charge. The thought popped into my mind even as I felt my heart sink. *He can turn things around. Your faith and hope aren't in your attorney, but in your Savior.* I nodded my head, agreeing with my own thoughts. With renewed peace and confidence, I replied, "My report is from the Lord. God will have the last word in the outcome of my case."

———

As we entered the court chamber, I looked around for Alexandra. She was there, near the front, sitting alongside Pastor Bloom. I was already predisposed to like Pastor Bloom because of what he was doing for my family, but when I found out that he was a former Port Authority police officer and had written a letter to the judge assuring him that my Christian faith was real and that I was a transformed person, I felt deeply indebted.

On the other side of Alexandra sat Mami and Fabian holding on to Sam and Adam, looking hopeful. I only caught a quick glimpse of them before I was ushered to my spot beside my lawyer, but I was encouraged by their presence.

The courtroom was large and opulent. If I hadn't been so aware of the judge's eyes on me, I would have spent time looking around, taking it all in. Instead, I sat facing forward, ready to accept whatever outcome God had planned.

"Stand here, Mr. Mendoza." The bailiff motioned to a place in front of the judge. I reached the spot on the hardwood floor he pointed to and looked up. I felt very much as if I were at home plate waiting for a curve ball.

The prosecutor began his opening presentation. "Your Honor, as I stand here today to address the court on Mr. Mendoza's actions in this criminal case, I first and foremost want to say that whatever time you impose on the defendant, I hope he will continue to do out in society what he has been doing in the prison system."

I had to be hearing him wrong. He sounded very much like he was defending me. *This is the miracle we've asked God for!*

Mr. Nabel looked surprised but proceeded as planned. "Your Honor, Mr. Mendoza has been an exemplary inmate. He's accomplished much in his rehabilitation, helping others both academically and spiritually. Countless inmates flock to Mr. Mendoza's church services, and he has unselfishly given them hope and assistance. We see here, Your Honor, dozens of letters written by inmates on behalf of Mr. Mendoza asking the court to grant him leniency and favor." He laid a stack of letters in front of the judge. "In the letters submitted on behalf of Mr. Mendoza, fellow prisoners have clearly stated how Mr. Mendoza's counseling has helped them to keep on living when they wanted to end their lives. Your Honor, his wife and children are present, as well as his extended family and pastor. Please consider them in your decision. Thank you."

It was my turn to speak. I almost couldn't find my voice, I was so in awe of what God was doing. I chose to make it short and simple. What else was there left to say? "Your Honor, I'd like you to know that the man you're seeing today is not the same person of three and a half years ago. I am a new person in Christ, and if you grant me the opportunity to be integrated back into society, I will make a positive difference as a law-abiding citizen."

The judge's face was unreadable. He shifted slightly in his chair and gave a brief nod. "Is that all you have to say?" His tone was dismissive, as if my case was of no importance to him.

"Yes, Your Honor."

He raised his gavel. "I hereby sentence you to forty-eight months of prison time with a probation term of five years." With a brief tap of that little wooden hammer, it was over.

I had already served forty-one months at MDC, Brooklyn, which meant I only had seven months left! After almost four years of anticipating the worst, I was met with a better outcome than any of us had dared to hope for.

I wanted to whoop and holler and dance a jig. I would be home in no time! A deep sense of gratitude flooded me. *God, you're so good. Thank you! Thank you for your mercy.*

Back at 5-North, I went looking for Emilio. I found him still on his knees, praying for my trial. I am sure he knew the outcome was good by the glee on my face. "So? Tell me."

"Man, Emilio, it was a miracle. God totally answered our prayers!" I told him how much time I had left with probation.

His mouth fell open. "That's it?"

"That's it!"

Emilio shook his head in awe. "Incredible. That is a miracle. You know that, right?"

I grinned. "We need to pray for a similar outcome for you now."

Emilio's sentencing was still three months away, but for the first time in a very long time, he too had hope that he would soon be free.

I had about a week and a half between my sentencing and my transfer to a new facility where I would serve out the last of my six months. It gave me time to say good-bye to the guys in 5-North. I was excited to be moving one step closer to freedom, but it was hard to leave my Christian brothers. God had done some amazing things there. The guys had become like family, and I would miss them.

Saying good-bye to Emilio was harder. I pulled him into a hug. "Keep on leading in faith."

"You know I will."

I felt a lump grow in my throat as his tears wet my shoulder. As I left, I prayed, *God please, raise up other inmates to pastor that little ragtag group of redeemed misfits once Emilio and I leave.*

37

ALLENWOOD

I arrived at Federal Correctional Institution Allenwood Low in Pennsylvania, excited to have a clear view of God's creations: the large leafy trees, the thick grass, the deer gamboling in the golden morning mist. The change from a high-security facility in the city to a low-security facility in the country was drastic. Allenwood had only a single barbed wire fence surrounding the perimeter—no more walls.

The few months I had left to go until my release would be spent in relative ease.

"I'm afraid we're overpacked, and there are no beds in general population. You'll have to spend the next few days in the SHU."

The officer processing the intakes sounded almost apologetic. Almost.

SHU, or solitary confinement, stood for Special Housing Unit and was for people with high-profile cases. It was also where troubled inmates were sent if they'd committed a violent crime and needed to be separated from the general inmate population.

I wanted to argue that I had been reclassified as low security, but I doubted my pleas would make any difference. They had no room. What was he supposed to do about it?

Another officer came and handcuffed me. "This way."

I followed him through a maze of hallways to a tiny cell with only enough space for a bunk bed and a toilet. A tiny Plexiglas window high in the wall let light through, but it was so scratched and warped that it was impossible to make sense of the view beyond. Deflated, I sat on the bunk and wondered what to do with myself.

There seemed to be two options: Sit on my bunk and read, or take a nap. I opened my Bible and started reading. It should have been easy to concentrate, since there were absolutely no distractions, but I found that the quiet itself distracted me. I wondered how long I could be locked up in there alone before going crazy.

Luckily, I didn't have to find out. A few hours later another inmate was brought in.

"I'm Herman." I offered my hand once his cuffs were removed.

"Sharif."

"What are you in for?"

"A credit card scheme. Now they're deporting me. Can you believe it? I've been in America since I was a kid." Sharif looked ticked.

"Where are you from originally?"

"Pakistan. Two decades here in the States, but they want to send me to a place I barely remember."

You get to know a guy real fast when he's the only person you can talk to. Even faster when you share an open toilet. Sharif and I agreed on a copacetic arrangement: If one of us had to go, the other would hold up a bedsheet to offer some privacy.

Sharif really liked to talk, and he had a lot to say about the US government. After an hour-long tirade, his anger seemed to subside and he sank back onto the bunk. "What about you, Herman? What's your story?"

I told him how I ended up serving time, but inevitably I focused on how God changed me in MDC. "It feels so good to know all the dirt and all the crap I had been involved in is forgiven."

He gave a low whistle. "I wish that's how it worked for me, but I'm a Muslim."

"Really? I studied a bit about Islam. Did you know the Koran talks about Jesus?"

Sharif's eyes widened in surprise.

"It's true. It shares some of His teachings and reveres Him as a prophet. But—here's something else that is interesting—the Holy Bible doesn't mention Muhammad at all. It warns against anyone that might take the place of Jesus in our life. It says that Jesus is the only way to have a relationship with God."

"Huh. That is kinda interesting." He flipped over on his side to look at me. "You know, I've never been very religious. I believe there is a God, but I never really paid Him much attention. I never heard anyone say that God made them a new person. I'm not sure I even know what you mean. Why did God do that for you?"

"It's not something God did just for me. The Bible says God offers that new life to all who believe and make Him the Lord of their lives. He did the same thing in my brother, and my wife, and countless other guys in 5-North."

"No kidding?"

"No kidding."

We spent three days in the SHU together before a bed opened up, but it felt much longer. I felt close to Sharif; I deeply wanted him to know Jesus so that even if this was the last time I saw him on this earth, I might see him again in heaven.

I'd barely stepped foot in my new unit when a tall Hispanic man greeted me. "Hello. Praise the Lord. Welcome! Name's Robert Garcia." His eyes flicked to the Bible tucked between my arm and my duffel bag. "Are you a Christian?"

I grinned. "I am, yes." Garcia's eyes crinkled when he smiled, and his voice was warm and inviting. He led me to an open cubicle. There were no cells in this unit—just cubicles about four feet high with beds on either side. They were single cots and not bunk beds, which was a plus. There were no doors and no privacy, but it was miles better than the SHU.

That evening, Robert stopped by with some toiletries and food. It was just like the welcome baskets our church in 5-North had put together.

"We have Bible study tonight in one of the cubicles. Would you like to come?" he asked.

"Yes! Definitely."

After just two hours, I had already found a church family.

———

"My wife's asking me for a divorce," Robert confessed one day as we talked. "I think she's having an affair. The only reason I can come up with for her wanting a divorce all of a sudden is some other guy pressuring her to leave me."

I knew what the poor man was feeling. "The same thing happened to me, but my wife gave her life to the Lord, and it completely saved our marriage. I'm gonna start praying, and I'll talk to my wife. Maybe she could speak to your wife and share our story with her."

A few days later I spoke to Alexandra over the phone.

"Have you seen the weather?" Alexandra asked. "I'm going to cancel our trip to the amusement park today and visit you instead."

I found Robert in his cubicle. "My wife is coming to visit me today. Do you think your wife is coming too?"

He shook his head. "I doubt it."

I sank down beside him. "I think we need to pray about this. We need to remember that God is in control. We can wait on Him and His perfect timing."

———

"Mendoza! Garcia! You have visitors."

My stomach jumped at the call. One bonus of a low-security prison was being able to sit together with your visitor. We were even allowed to kiss our spouses when they arrived.

In the visiting area, I rushed to Alexandra and took full advantage of the kissing rule.

Robert stared at a woman who had to be Mrs. Garcia. I suggested the four of us sit together, and Alexandra and I took turns sharing our story.

"It's really only Jesus giving me the power to forgive Herman," Alexandra explained. "I thought I had been hurt too much and the damage was irreparable, but I was wrong. I want you to know that God loves you so much that He changed the weather so that I could cancel my plans with my kids to be here with you."

Mrs. Garcia began to cry. "I've been a fool." She wiped the tears from her cheeks, and Alexandra handed her a Kleenex. "I just didn't want to see the truth. . . . I thought I would be risking more hurt." She glanced over at Robert, her expression no longer hard or cold.

"I can pray with you if you'd like," I told her. "Do you want to repent and receive God's forgiveness?"

She nodded. I led her in a prayer almost identical to the one I had prayed with Alexandra.

Right there, in that visiting area, her broken heart was restored.

She met Robert's eyes. "I think that God has good plans for us."

Robert's joy spilled over in great tears as he uttered, "Please forgive me. I know I haven't been a perfect husband."

Alexandra and I grinned as we watched them embrace at the end of the visit. It was incredible to see God do for the Garcias what He had done for us.

A few days later, I got a letter from Alexandra.

God is so good to let us join the work He's doing in people's lives. We should think about starting something together when you get out. Wouldn't it be great to be in a full-time ministry together?

Over the next few months, our letters and calls always included plans and ideas for a future ministry together. We'd call it Stepping Stones Ministries. Our mission was to work with families that had been devastated by natural disaster or incarceration. We would provide youth and family counseling, as well as healing through the Word of God.

One day in chapel, a guy from another unit approached me. He held out his hand. "I hear you're the preacher man."

"That's what they call me."

"Daniel McCarthy. I wanted to meet a fellow brother in Christ."

"How did you end up here?"

He motioned for me to sit down, a sign that it was going to be a long story. We sat together on a hard chapel bench.

"I always believed in God," he said. "But back before my days here, I never did much about it. I believed that as long as I tried to live a good life I was fine.

"Thing is, I liked money . . . a lot. I thought as long as I gave a certain amount of money to good causes, it probably didn't matter to God where I got it from. So I set up a Ponzi scheme. I swindled over $500 million from investors. I'm only sure of that figure because it seems the feds kept better records than I did."

I knew firsthand how meticulous the feds were.

"I'm glad now that I got caught. God got ahold of me here, and I realized no matter how much I tried to justify or pretty-up my sin, it was still sin. Stealing was stealing, no matter what I did with the money. Once I recognized my sin and repented, God made me a new man."

"Yes! That's exactly how God works, isn't it?" I said. "Do you know what you're going to do when you get out?"

He rubbed at his chin as he gave it some consideration.

"I guess I don't. I'm working on a theology degree right now, though, and I know God's going to lead me."

It was the start of several good conversations over the following weeks. Talking to Daniel was like talking to a best friend, but I got the sense that Daniel was holding back something he wanted to say. I was curious, but I didn't want to push him.

Finally, during a short pause in one of our talks, he blurted, "I believe God has given me a message for you. He wants you to know that you will be an ambassador for God's kingdom. You will be traveling around the world. You will meet public figures that will render their services to you for the advancement of the kingdom of God.

"You will deliver humanitarian aid. You will help many young people and those that are in gangs and doing drugs to come to know Christ. You will shape the lives of many with your testimony."

A zing of excitement ran through me. Could that be true? Something in my spirit said *yes*. I didn't know the specifics, but I believed and trusted that whenever the time was right, I would be ready.

38

A Test of Faith

The months in Allenwood passed, and the time for my release arrived. I couldn't have been more excited; it was the day I had been dreaming of for the last four years. Alexandra had sent me a going-away outfit.

I had just finished changing when two officers came into the holding pen. They looked like they meant business.

"Herman Mendoza. There's a warrant for your arrest. We will be escorting you to Rikers Island." A detainer had been issued due to my parole violation, allowing them to keep me in prison longer.

The happy butterflies in my stomach turned to lead weights. I was dumbfounded! *God, what do I do? What's happening?*

Immediately, a sense of calm washed over me. *God must have plans for me at Rikers.*

The uniformed officers showed a surprising amount of compassion as they handcuffed me and escorted me to their vehicle; perhaps they saw the gray pallor of disappointment wash over me.

The landscape of the island was desolate—nothing but jails as far as the eye can see.

The conditions in the state jail were so much worse than in federal facilities. And it wasn't just because of funding. Federal prisons tended to house criminals like me and my brothers—men who sold drugs but rarely got their hands dirty. Men like Daniel McCarthy, who masterminded Ponzi schemes or conducted large-scale heists. But each state prison on the island housed a collection of the most dangerous inmates in New York.

We arrived at one of the ten jails, EMTC. On a totally different area of the island from where I was housed before, EMTC was a neglected facility for inmates with impending cases or parole and probation violations.

I was processed and taken to a holding pen filled with drug addicts. These hopeless men broke my heart. How many people like these had been my onetime customers? *God, thank you for changing me. Help me to show these men your love and point them to freedom. Their futures don't have to be hopeless.* I reminded myself that I could speak words of hope in this hopeless place.

Some of the guys in holding listened as I told them the stories from my years in 5-North. They became intrigued by the power of God.

Hours later, my name was called, and I was escorted to the housing unit. I scanned the area, hoping to see someone I could connect with, but it didn't look promising. *God, please show me your purpose for me here.*

I glanced around, half expecting an immediate answer. No one approached me. No one in particular caught my eye.

Maybe tomorrow.

Tonight I would take a shower, have a good sleep, and get ready for whatever God asked me to do.

"Hey, preacher!" An inmate known for selling drugs in the prison edged up to me in the rec area. "I've been hearing your story. Can we talk?"

Quite a few guys were looking at us, wondering what the preacher and the dealer had to talk about.

"Over here." He motioned for me to follow him to a place near the officer's booth in the center of the unit. None of the inmates wanted to hang out there, so it offered a decent amount of privacy.

In a whisper, he said, "I hear there's a lot of guys coming by your bunk for Bible studies."

I nodded.

"I wanna change too. I gotta quit this lifestyle and give my life to God, just like you."

I almost burst out laughing—not because it was funny but because the thought of this man being transformed by Jesus filled me with so much joy that my body couldn't contain it. Instead of laughing, I said, "That's awesome! I can pray with you."

He raised a hand to stop me. "The problem is the money is too good—even in jail. I'm making more in here than I can outside. How can I walk away?"

Money. Greed. Old Herman knew the allure all too well, but it amazed me how much Jesus had changed me. It really didn't have the same hold on me anymore. "Listen man," I said, "the money, the material stuff you're chasing after, it won't satisfy. I've been there. I've done that. You're chasing after chains, man. It will enslave you." I shared with him the words that had made all the difference in my life. "Jesus came to set the captives free. He can take those desires and transform them. He can place new, healthy desires in your heart. The best life you can have is with Christ."

Conversations like these, I realized, were God's purpose for me on Rikers.

After two months on the island, I had a visit from my attorney.

"The parole board has set a court date to hear your case. Since you violated your conditional release last time, it sounds like you're looking at another three years in prison. If you hadn't, I think we could have gotten you out right away."

It wasn't what I'd hoped to hear, but I understood. I was a bail jumper who'd set up a false business to hide my illegal activities while on parole. And I'd been caught. I deserved it.

The day of my hearing was ushered in with sunshine and cloudless skies.

A smiling Philip Nabel updated me on my case. "I feel good about this one, Herman. I've submitted all the paper work to the judge, and I'm hopeful that I can get you reinstated in supervised parole."

Please, Lord, let him be right.

By this time, I had spent two months on Rikers Island, pending the outcome of my case. The hearing took place in a trailer-style portable office.

The judge gave me a quick once over. "Mr. Mendoza." His voice was nasal with a strong New York accent. "You've done great things in prison and have been shown to be rehabilitated."

Suddenly, his voice sounded sweet, almost melodious.

"I hereby grant your reinstatement as a parolee, and you are released back into society. I wish you much success."

39

No Turning Back

The next day, I heard a loud voice from the corridor. "Time to go!" Two guards escorted me to a holding area while they ran a background check for any outstanding warrants.

Fear rose up in my throat. *Is it possible they'll find something I haven't served time for again?* "Lord," I prayed, "I just want go home to my family. Please, please let this process go smoothly."

They motioned me forward. "Here's your transit card and some money for a call."

I exhaled the breath I didn't know I was holding. At last, I was free to go.

I walked through the waiting area past multiple security checkpoints and found the public phone. For the first time in years, I held a phone against my ear without the weight and clink of handcuffs on my wrists.

Alexandra was waiting at my parents' place with the kids. As I dialed the familiar number, I noticed a little leaflet sitting on top of the phone box. I tucked the phone between my ear and shoulder and picked it up. Emblazoned across the top were the words "Choose this day whom you will serve. As for me and my house, we will serve the Lord."* This couldn't be a coincidence. It was a word from God, a reminder that as long as I followed Him, I would never go back to my old life.

*From Joshua 24:15 ESV

Mami picked up the phone, her familiar "¿Sí, hola?" like music to my ears.

"Mami! It's me, Herman. I'm free. I'm out!"

"Praise God! Praise God!" There were laughter and tears in her voice. "Did you want to speak to Alexandra?"

I was torn between not wanting to hang up and wanting to get home as soon as possible. "¡Sí! Mami, gracias."

The phone rattled as she placed it on the table. It was really late, and I could hear her walk toward my old room and wake Alexandra. They were probably all exhausted. It had been a long day of waiting. I'd be exhausted too, if I wasn't feeling so much like a kid at Christmas.

I heard Mami pick up the receiver again and pass it to Alexandra. Before she could speak, I cried out, "I love you, Alexandra. I'll be home soon."

Alexandra started sobbing in response. I could hear Mami crying in the background too. Happy tears.

I passed security checkpoints, pushed through several turnstile gates, and found myself looking up at the orange glow of city lights. Right beside the entrance was the bus stop. I fished out the public transit card, really looking at it for the first time. It was different than I'd remembered.

A lot had changed since I had been in the pen. I had spent the turn of the millennium behind bars. I remembered when the year 2000 seemed like a futuristic time, when people would have flying cars and robots that cleaned your house. We didn't quite get there, but there were technologies now I couldn't have dreamed of as a kid. Two years into the new millennium and mobile phones had cameras and access to the internet. People listened to music on little devices called MP3 players. Everything was smaller and sleeker. The world had changed so much in just under five years.

The city bus pulled up with a familiar metallic screech. I scanned my transit card and found a seat. My knees wouldn't stop shaking. My mind knew I was a free man, but I felt very much like I was escaping. I kept glancing over my shoulder to reassure myself that no one was chasing after me.

I pulled out the leaflet I'd found on top of the phone. The words reassured me that I wasn't going back to Queens alone. I went back as a child of God. I fished in my pocket for a pen and scribbled on the leaflet, *This is the first thing I saw when I got out.* Then I tucked it back into my wallet. I'd keep it as a constant reminder of what God had done.

Behind me was the gloominess of concrete walls and barbed wire fences, and I was moving toward hope and a future.

Black against the midnight-blue sky was the familiar outline of the row houses in the old neighborhood. Mami and Alexandra rushed out onto the street, hugged me close, and kissed me before leading me back into the house.

The front entrance still smelled of oiled wood. It's funny how you can forget the smell of home, but when you smell it again it's so familiar that it brings with it a million memories. I was overcome with nostalgia as Mami and Alexandra pushed me through the second door and into the hallway. A large banner was strung across it. "¡Bienvenido, Herman!" Welcome home. It was a more beautiful welcome than I could have dreamed.

"Sit down at the table." Mami led me toward the dining room. "I've made you moro de habichuela negra." She had cooked the Dominican dishes I had missed so much: fried sweet plantains, baked chicken, rice and black beans. The midnight feast made the whole house smell great.

When my stomach couldn't take any more, I thanked Mami, took a quick shower, and then headed to bed. Down the hallway, past the kitchen, was my old bedroom. I tried to be quiet as I pushed open the door. The light from the hallway illuminated the beautiful faces of my children. Samantha had matured so much. Where was my little girl? And Adam—he wasn't a toddler anymore. But I was so grateful to God that since they were eleven and eight, I hadn't missed their entire childhoods. Tears of joy rolled down my face. *I'm going to be the father you never had—a man who loves God and takes care of his family*, I vowed silently, bending to kiss them.

"Daddy?" Sam's eyes, suddenly alert, studied my face.

I had half hoped the kids would wake up. I pulled her close.

Adam woke seconds later. "Daddy! Daddy!"

He climbed into my arms as well, and we sat there for a long time. They didn't stop hugging and kissing me, and I didn't want them to stop.

It was almost an hour later when they finally drifted back to sleep. I lay down beside Alexandra on the little single bed on the opposite side of the room. "I love you, Alexandra. I love our little family."

She sighed happily and pecked my cheek. "Things are going to be okay from now on. You'll see. God is going to do great things for us."

40

Freshman Year

Alexandra's eyes glistened with tears as she looked at me. "I, Alexandra, take you, Herman, to be my husband. To love and to cherish until death do us part."

I had to swallow the lump in my throat before I could respond. "I, Herman, take you, Alexandra, to be my wife. To love and to cherish until death do us part."

I pulled my wife into my arms and kissed her before we got on our knees beside our hotel bed and asked God to bless and sanctify our marriage. We were starting fresh, dedicating our lives and love to God so that we could move forward in His purposes.

When we got to our feet, Alexandra pulled me back into a hug. "This was a blessing. Thank you."

I kissed her again. "I love you. I can't wait to see where God moves us next."

———

My first year as a free man went by in a flash, likely because there were so many changes. One of the most urgent requirements of my parole was to find a job. My attorney had mentioned that they were looking for a paralegal and that my knowledge of the law could be a real asset. I couldn't say no to an offer like that.

But as much as I enjoyed helping our clients at Nabel and Schwartz, Attorneys at Law, it felt like there was something lacking. As the months passed I started to feel emptier and emptier.

I talked it over with Alexandra, and we weighed the pros and cons. She reminded me of the shared vision God had given us when I was still in prison: Stepping Stones Ministries, our very own organization that focused on reaching prisoners and children and youth with the gospel, as well as providing relief aid to victims of natural disasters. Alexandra and her nephew Raynier had even created a logo.

"If I get a better paying job, I can bring in enough for rent and bills and you can focus on full-time ministry," Alexandra suggested.

I gave her a hug. "I can't believe how blessed I am that God has given me you for a wife."

———

By the summer of 2003, I was still out of work and funds were tight. I had left the paralegal job to pursue full-time ministry. Although we had begun to see some promise in Stepping Stones Ministries, it provided no income.

That season was possibly the biggest test of my faith and commitment to God since I'd been released. We sometimes wondered if we would be able to feed our kids.

After a while, Alexandra started to wonder if we had heard God correctly. "I'm not saying you shouldn't be in full-time ministry, but maybe you should try to find work with some of the bigger Christian organizations here."

I was willing to try, but as I applied to various places it became clear that I wasn't going to find employment that way either.

Thank God for mentors like Reverend Ricksy. He empathized with our struggles and helped put food on our table. He didn't let me wallow in self-pity. "You believed God called you to start Stepping Stones, so you have an obligation to work hard at it. And don't worry about how it will work out. Trust God to take it where He wants it to go."

It was sage advice. Eventually, Stepping Stones started to build a base of supporters, enough for a small salary. It wasn't a living wage, but it was something.

Our ministry to local youth started with basketball camps as a means of reaching inner-city kids. They were a big hit. Kids flocked to them. We had all sorts of opportunities to walk alongside hurting kids who were going through some really difficult times.

As Stepping Stones grew, we started recruiting. Robert Garcia, newly released from prison, joined our team and expanded the prison ministry.

Emilio had been released from prison a few months after I was. He wondered what sort of ministry God would have him do. "What do you think about starting a newspaper?" he asked one day.

We weren't journalists. We had no media background of any kind, but if we wanted to evangelize in a big way, a newspaper seemed an optimal way to do it. It might also help us make valuable connections to grow Stepping Stones.

The Mendoza brothers were back in business.

"Your daughter wants to see you."

I hadn't expected to hear Daria's voice when I picked up the phone. But it wasn't a bad surprise; I wanted to see Penelope as well.

From the sound of things, Daria was still the woman I had known before. Her relationship with Penelope had not turned out to be the best. I wondered if I might be able to convince her and Alexandra to let Penelope live with us instead.

When I hung up with Daria, I talked to Alexandra about it. "What should we do? It's not good for her to grow up in that environment. She's at a vulnerable age, and I worry she's going to make some very bad choices."

Alexandra nodded, slowly, thoughtfully.

"Maybe she could live with us, here in a Christian home."

"Yeah, I think that's a wonderful idea," Alexandra said. "I would really love that."

It took Samantha and Adam a little while to get used to having another sibling in their lives. But the three of them got along really well. Once Penelope moved in, our family felt complete. It was hard to imagine a time when she wasn't with us.

Running our newly minted newspaper, the *Trinity Tribune*, didn't detract from my youth ministry in Queens. If anything, it complemented it well.

The youth program had already created a buzz with the local ministers who feared their young people would end up in prison. They saw that this ministry was changing lives. Soon the buzz wasn't just in Christian circles. Local politicians and city officials heard about the events and invited us to lead community outreaches.

Over the next few months or so, Emilio and I were featured in the *New York Daily News, Newsday, TimesLedger*, a short film by Time Warner's Doculab, and Trinity Broadcasting Network (TBN). And the requests kept coming.

Interviews led to invitations to speak at various events. Suddenly, I was telling my story at Christian conferences and banquets, schools and churches, Jewish youth programs, and Fortune 500 companies.

Emilio and I were ecstatic. God was giving us a platform to tell the world how He had saved us.

"Herman, we gotta ask God how He wants us to move forward," Emilio said as we planned our next issue of the *Trinity Tribune*. "I keep feeling like God wants to do bigger and greater things than we have been doing."

As soon as Emilio said the words, my spirit confirmed them. The news was covering a flash flood that hit the Dominican Republic and Haiti, claiming the lives of more than two thousand people, and my heart ached for them. And I wondered if maybe what Emilio and I were feeling was God calling us to go international.

I called up one of our interns, a talented photographer with a good grasp on what made a story interesting. "Corey, I want to send you to Jimani in D.R. We need some pictures of the destruction, and I'd like it if you could bring us some stories from the people there."

A few days later, I looked over the photographs Corey had sent back. The interviews broke my heart. People already living in impoverished conditions had been left with nothing.

One story in particular affected all of us. A woman, eight months pregnant, was asleep in her hut when the rains came. Just before the floodwaters reached her, she awoke to a mighty roaring. As she tried to make sense of what was going on, the full force of the floodwaters crashed against her home. She scrambled to get out of bed, but it was too late. The force of the waters took out everything in its path, dragging the expectant mother hundreds of feet before consuming other buildings in the town. Remarkably, she survived.

Her story stirred something in me. If we told it, and told it well, I believed others would be moved too. And if we all came together, we could effect real change.

41

Missions

Sometimes God prepares you for a task before you have an inkling that you'll need the training. The original vision for Stepping Stones included relief aid, so when I saw an advertisement for a chaplaincy preparedness course for lay ministers in New York City, I immediately signed up. It was led by the Billy Graham Evangelistic Association, and it wrapped up just before Hurricane Katrina hit.

I found myself joining the Billy Graham Evangelistic Association's relief efforts in New Orleans. There was a lot to do, and the work was incredibly fulfilling.

More and more, I felt like God had something prepared for me and He was guiding me into it, teaching and training me along the way.

Two countries close to my heart, Haiti and the Dominican Republic, were making headlines. Tensions along the Dominican-Haitian border were increasing. Haitians tried to cross the border illegally in hopes of finding food and supplies that were sadly lacking on their side, and tempers ignited on the Dominican side as farmers and villagers fought to protect their businesses.

Around this same time, I heard about a global network of medical and health professionals and volunteers dedicated to alleviating human suffering. They already had a contact in the United Nations that helped them partner with hospitals and pharmaceutical companies that donated millions of dollars' worth of goods. Rather than struggle to establish our ministry to do the same thing, I partnered with them. Suddenly, I had the ability to send large amounts of humanitarian aid to the Dominican Republic and Haiti.

The organization had celebrity advocates, who leveraged their platforms to garner support. One of the celebrity advocates was Haitian-American hip-hop musician Wyclef Jean.

Through the organization, I was introduced to Wyclef. It was great to work with this man who had such a passion for his people in Haiti. Our partnership showed that a Haitian-American and a Dominican-American can work together and led us to form a new movement called One Voice, which sought to bring peace between Haitians and Dominicans and provided aid to the island that both countries called home.

"You're invited to go to the UN?" Alexandra was incredulous.

Never in my wildest dreams would I have thought I would be going to the United Nations someday. But it was happening. I was invited to be a representative of the work in Haiti. God had not only placed in me a deep desire to reach the people of Hispaniola, He had provided the means and opportunity.

"What will you wear?"

I tried to act like I didn't care much what I wore, but I already had a suit picked out.

Saying yes to God was leading me on greater adventures than I'd ever had as a drug dealer. If someone had told me ten years before that I would be a Bible-thumping, do-gooder Christian, I would have laughed in his face. But here I was representing God on the world stage.

Once again, God led me to the people and places that could help me. This time to Alice Mora, a student at Columbia University and an outspoken advocate for peace on the Haitian-Dominican border.

She heard about my work and invited me to speak at an open forum on Dominican-Haitian relations at the School of Social Work.

Also attending the event were the UN ambassador of the Dominican Republic and Raymond Joseph, a former Haitian ambassador to the United States.

Raymond and I found that God had given us both a vision to see Haitians and Dominicans reconcile. Raymond's cousin also just happened to be Wyclef Jean—yet another connection. After that night, we often chatted on the phone about ways to reach our countries with the message of peace. Wyclef, being something of a celebrity, seemed the ideal person to headline events, so we planned things around his schedule to bring positive PR to the project.

I also met Bienvenido Lopez at the forum. We became close friends, connecting over the shared belief that sin was the main cause of conflict between both countries. We knew that if people from both sides would repent and make God the Lord of their lives, the entire island of Hispaniola would be changed.

Together, Bienvenido and I created a plan to organize a prayer rally alongside the Dajabón River, more commonly called the Massacre River. The river got its nickname in the 1700s, when thirty French buccaneers were murdered there by Spanish settlers. The name was reinforced in 1937, when under the command of Rafael Trujillo, thousands of Haitians were slaughtered on its banks. Our goal was to change what that river was known for.

"Imagine," Bienvenido said with wonder in his voice, "if instead of the Massacre River it was renamed the River of Peace!"

When we had done all we could from the United States to organize the prayer rally, I took a group to the Dominican Republic, including Bienvenido; Robert Garcia; Cliff, a young Haitian-American man I had met at a Christian hip-hop concert; and some Christian artists.

As soon as we got off the plane, it was all systems go. We had just ten days to pull it all together.

A press conference at the El Jaragua Hotel, one of the most well-known and prestigious hotels in Santo Domingo, was our first stop. Reporters from the mainstream media were there waiting to hear from us.

As clearly and simply as possible, I said, "Our goal is to call for a day of prayer and spiritual unity, where we can pray for one another and for peace and tranquility alongside the border that separates our two countries."

Nine days later, Robert Garcia, Cliff, Brenda—a woman who had helped us organize the conference—and I loaded up a truck with all our equipment and headed for the border.

It was evening by the time we got there. The border guards warned us that we had only thirty minutes before they closed the gates for the night. Once the gates were closed they couldn't open them again until morning.

"What should we do?" I asked.

"Thirty minutes isn't long. We have to cross the bridge, unload, and drive all the way back." Robert seemed a little worried.

"I think we'll have enough time if we hustle," Cliff said.

Brenda agreed.

"Okay . . . let's do this."

We passed through the gates and drove onto the bridge.

"Man, it's so dangerous . . . we can't stop for anything," our driver warned. "I really don't want to get stuck over there. It's so dark on that side. They don't have any lights."

His knuckles were white as he stopped and gripped the steering wheel. "You get stuck on that side, and they'll chop you up."

Just then, I heard the click of the passenger's side door. I looked over. Robert was missing.

Cliff, Brenda, the driver, and I all looked back to see Robert running at full speed back to the gate. I couldn't stop laughing. Robert wasn't a natural runner. He didn't even seem like much of a risk taker, but he'd rather jump out of a moving vehicle than get caught on the Haitian side of border control.

Just a few miles away from the lush green shrubs of the Dominican Republic, the Haitian landscape looked desolate. One island, two totally different worlds.

We didn't waste any time while unloading the equipment. We may not have been as gentle as we could have been. Despite chuckling at Robert when he bailed on us, I wasn't eager to stay overnight there either.

We didn't make it. We were only five minutes late, but the gates were closed and locked. We parked and locked the truck.

We begged the guards on the Dominican side to let us through.

"Come on," Brenda pleaded, "just call the general. We can give you his number. We're having an event over there tomorrow."

The guard shook his head.

"What if we just climbed over, and you looked the other way?" I asked.

The guard gave me a little thumbs-up and a nod.

The only way we could actually get across was if we climbed over the side of the fence in the middle of the bridge and down onto the side rails without falling into the river. The river was commonly used by Haitians to deal with sewage, and it was full of all sorts of disease. But we didn't really have any other choice.

The four of us climbed the fence, traversing the barbed wire as delicately as possible. Next came the hard part. We dropped down on top of the side rails of the bridge and inched our way along it. Mosquitoes buzzed in our ears and swarmed our exposed flesh, but we had no free hands to slap them away.

The unbearable heat of the day hadn't lessened with the evening. My whole body felt like it was dripping. Everything felt slippery as I clung with all my might. And then, it was over. We had made it.

I wanted to laugh or cry . . . or both.

On the day of the prayer rally, thousands crossed the border into Haiti together, thanks to the friendly immigration officials and probably some divine intervention.

It was a sight to behold. Haitians and Dominicans together, peacefully praying and praising God.

Cliff opened his performance with a song he wrote just for the event. As he sang, we asked some children to come up on stage with us and release white doves as a symbol of peace.

As I prayed, I felt the presence of God rest on me strongly.

The gathering prayed and called on the name of Jesus. We danced and sang, celebrating the unity that was ours in Christ. The atmosphere was awesome, in the true sense of the word. Almost overwhelming.

The morning after the prayer rally, we tuned in to the news. They were calling it "a wonderful day of prayer for unity."

"Isn't it amazing how God brought us together?" I thanked each one of them, especially Robert for his financial support of this cause.

***

I had to admit, my heart for ministry was growing and my interest in business was shrinking. What was the use of spending time on things that weren't advancing God's kingdom?

Our newspaper was doing well, we had covered stories at home and abroad, but it just didn't seem like it was as important a ministry as my work in Haiti and the Dominican Republic and with the youth.

I had made some great contacts with world leaders and ambassadors as a result of the prayer rally and my work with local organizations.

***

Some called Armando Batista peculiar, but I thought he was hilarious. A court officer working as a captain in the New York State Supreme Court Building in Manhattan, Batista was hard to miss with a big personality to match his six-foot-three frame. We first met through a chaplaincy program in Brooklyn.

"You know, I was thinking I should introduce you to some of my friends," Batista said one day over coffee. "Most of them are presiding judges, and I think they would be really interested in your youth programs."

Batista took me to meet Judge Donna Mills. She greeted us with a warm smile, her eyes attentive, analytical, perceptive. I could tell she was using her judicial expertise to examine me.

In a fraction of a second, she had passed judgment on me and showed her approval, as if she had seen in me something she could trust.

Her smile broadened as I talked about the work I was currently doing with the local youth and in Haiti. I told her the stories of the people who had touched my heart. They seemed to resonate with her. At the end of our visit, she held out her business card. "If there's anything you need, give me a call."

In the following months, we got to know each other much better. True to her word she was ready and willing to help. Not only did she donate to our organization, she also became a family friend.

Partnering with Batista in ministry was pretty cool. A now retired captain and an ex-con together sharing how God had changed their lives.

42

A New Direction

It was January 2010, and Emilio's father-in-law was dying of cancer. My brother and I sat by his hospital bed praying for comfort and peace. As we kept vigil, waiting for God to carry this man home, a news report on his little hospital television caught our attention.

"A massive earthquake, measuring 7.0 on the Richter scale, has just rocked the Caribbean nation of Haiti. . . . The Red Cross is reporting that over three million people have been affected."

Crowding my thoughts as the report continued was how the people of Haiti had already suffered so much. The earthquake was catastrophic. Already in the first hour, they were reporting thousands dead.

The counter for the death toll, which ran along the bottom of the screen, looked like a stopwatch. More fatalities were added with every second. In those same moments, Emilio's father-in-law breathed his last.

When I got home, I found Alexandra sitting silently in front of the television. She barely registered my arrival. "Oh Herman, it's terrible. So many . . . bodies."

I sat next to her and hugged her close. She put her head on my shoulder and looked up at me. "What are we going to do about our trip?"

We had booked a flight to Haiti not long ago for one of our regular ministry trips. Now the trip took on a different tone.

"Should we postpone until we can go with more supplies?"

My brain was still catching up with all that was happening. "I'm not sure, but when we go we need to bring whatever, and whomever we can."

It had been a hard month for us. Not only had Emilio's father-in-law just passed away, but we had transitioned our newspaper company into a digital advertisement company, and that month it was lost in a fire.

"You know, Herman," Alexandra said, "I've been praying a lot about what God's been allowing in our lives. I couldn't understand it at first—why the business had burned down. But I think He allowed this to happen because He wants us to be in full-time ministry. Our focus shouldn't be divided anymore."

"I think that is exactly what God is doing," I agreed.

Not long after we prayed together, asking God for direction, I got a call from a friend, a chiropractor who often participated in the humanitarian group Chiropractors Without Borders. "Herman, I hope you can help us. My group is trying to get into Haiti, but we keep hitting roadblocks. Do you have contacts there? Can you get us in? We want to help."

"No problem. In fact, you're an answer to my prayers."

Four days after the earthquake, we drove rented SUVs across the Dominican-Haitian border. The cars were loaded with life-saving supplies, bottled water, food, and protein bars.

It was different traveling with the group of chiropractic professionals. Many of them had never been to places like this. "Just a word of warning," I called out to the group. "As we travel, you are going to see all sorts of roadside vendors. The food will look and smell delicious, but don't eat it unless you would like to experience Montezuma's revenge. It is much wiser to stick with the food we have brought with us."

A few laughed and a couple shrugged it off, but it seemed they forgot my warning. It didn't take long for their bodies to rebel and diarrhea to hit. That drive from Santo Domingo took us nine long, arduous hours. Three hours longer than it should have.

When we finally arrived at the border, massive lines of Haitians trying to flee the devastation crowded the Dominican immigration building. No one was trying to get into Haiti. It was like swimming against the current.

"It's strange there aren't more humanitarian aid trucks driving in," I told Alexandra. "Thank goodness the Dominican Red Cross is present."

As we got closer, the noise level increased. It sounded like a stadium full of screaming, crying masses. The faces of children, frightened and tear streaked, pressed into the shoulders of their parents who looked even more fearful and desperate than they did.

Military personnel lined the border, trying to bring order to the chaos while keeping back the hundreds—probably thousands—of Haitians trying to break through.

People pressed in around our vehicles, yelling in Creole. I didn't know what they were saying, but we could see they were desperate and likely begging for food.

Farther in was the rising stench of dead bodies. Everywhere you looked there were twisted limbs and ashen features peeking out from under the rubble.

There wasn't much help around, and there was no one to organize or direct.

We stopped our vehicles and tried to give out some water. Immediately, we were swarmed by masses of people grabbing and clutching for anything they could lay their hands on. Even as we struggled to bring some sort of order and assurance, we could see more crowds coming.

It wasn't safe to stay. We had to leave what we could and move on.

I thought of the desperation they must be feeling, and my emotions got the better of me. Death was all around, and the aftershocks kept coming.

I took out my camera to capture the images, hoping that when I took these stories back to the United States, more hearts would be broken for these people and more help would come.

Our first stop in Port-au-Prince was at the school: Institution Chrétienne de la Restauration. The head of the school was Bishop Pierre-Presler Dorcilien, whom I'd gotten to know when I first began working in Haiti in 2004. I hurt for him. I knew very well what it was like to lose your work in an instant. We canvassed the school, making sure it was empty of anyone still alive. All that remained was rubble.

After our stop at the school, we continued farther into the city. The stench of death was like a thick, enveloping fog all around us.

A few weeks later, Alexandra and I returned to the United States to organize more aid. Fortunately, I was contacted by a few news organizations, including Telemundo, a Spanish-language network, that asked me to share my experience.

I didn't hold back. I described in detail what we had seen and challenged viewers to give sacrificially to this devastated nation.

We visited Haiti again and again, often sending containers of medical supplies, food, clothing, and water ahead of us. But progress was slow. Red tape and corruption often made it difficult to collect our shipments once we arrived. Despite all the difficulties, though, we managed to deliver almost a million dollars' worth of goods to Haiti and see the Institution Chrétienne de la Restauration back up and running.

Later that year, Bishop Dorcilien helped conduct my ordination ceremony. I had felt a strong calling to be ordained as a pastor. I was reminded of the time I spent in prison and all those years studying the Bible. Promising to perform and uphold the duties and responsibilities that come with being an ordained pastor was fulfilling.

43

Promise Ministries International

"You lost your advertising business in that fire." There was worry in my friend Anthony's voice.

I had volunteered regularly at his youth basketball camp, and we had gotten to know each other well over the years.

"Are you okay financially?"

I couldn't lie—we weren't doing well at all. "God's been taking care of us day by day. We have all we need." I knew that was the Christian way of saying, "My life is kind of falling apart, actually." But in our case it was true. Yes, Alexandra and I would have loved to know how we were going to pay the bills each month. But when it came time, God always provided. "For the meantime," I told Anthony, "I know God wants me to focus on the task He called me to."

Anthony let out a sigh, as if my pain and worries were his own. "I'm going to be praying for you."

One day, I got a call from Anthony's father-in-law, Pete Richardson. "Anthony's been telling me about your youth ministry. In fact, I have been hearing a lot about you from members of my church as well. They've been telling me how committed you are, how you have helped so many of our kids and young people. We'd like you to come and speak at our church."

I was excited and agreed to speak at their church a few weeks later.

Alexandra and I drove to a local park to ask for God's guidance.

"Lord," I prayed, "please open the door for me to be able to support my family and to reach people for the sake of your kingdom. Grant me favor to work full-time in ministry. In Jesus' name, amen."

After we had finished praying we headed back home. Minutes later, my phone rang. It was Pastor Pete Richardson again. "My son-in-law Anthony mentioned that you were looking for work. I went ahead and recommended to the senior pastor of Promise Church, the Korean church we are affiliated with, to consider you for the role of leading our children's ministry, PowerHouse Kids. How about if we meet this week?"

How could this be anything but a God-given opportunity? I immediately agreed to come in for the interview.

I could barely contain my excitement when the day of the interview arrived. Alexandra and I really believed this was an opportunity from God for us.

I shook Pastor Richardson's hand. "Thanks again for calling me in."

"I am just glad you came. I really wanted you to meet Pastor Kim, the senior pastor at Promise Church. He's the one who will be interviewing you today. You might notice that you will have quite a lot of cultural differences."

Promise Church is a congregation with about five thousand members and three additional churches in Manhattan, New Jersey, and Georgia. But for some reason, I didn't feel nervous about the interview. I was so excited about a full-time ministry position that came with a steady income that I needed to remember not to try to sell myself. If this was really from God, He could do the sales pitch.

Pastor Kim's office was warm and welcoming. It felt intimate, more like a comfy living room than a workplace. Pastor Pete greeted Pastor Kim in a formal way before making introductions.

As Pastor Kim and I shook hands, I couldn't help but like him. Everything about him seemed pleasant and comfortable, as if I had known him for years. He exuded kindness and gentleness.

"Please," he said, "tell me about your background, Mr. Mendoza."

I talked about growing up in a Dominican neighborhood in Queens, which led us into a discussion on our cultures and history. Then I shared my testimony with Pastor Kim and explained what God had done for me. I was nervous about how he would react. Would he still consider me for this job?

When Pastor Kim and I had finished chatting, Pete interjected, "Pastor Kim and I were talking about bringing you on as part of the team leading PowerHouse Kids. You would be running the children's ministry every Saturday and offering free life-skills classes for different age groups."

I nodded. "That sounds really good."

Pastor Kim turned to Pete, shaking his head. "PowerHouse Kids is too small for Pastor Mendoza. I want him to work with me as my right-hand man for the 4/14 Window Global Movement."

I hadn't expected to be paired with the international youth outreach, but I wasn't opposed to it either.

Pastor Kim addressed me, "I want you to study this movement; we are just starting it. I'd like you to learn all you can."

Pete looked more surprised than I was at this unexpected turn. "But, Pastor Kim, we need him for PowerHouse Kids."

It felt good to know that both of these respected men thought me capable of working in this growing ministry. I assured them, "I am here to serve in any capacity. I can do both!"

Pastor Kim smiled, his eyes crinkling in a grandfatherly way. He pursed his lips and nodded in thought for just a moment. "Think and pray about it. If you want one job, or both, you can start right away."

"Yes sir, Pastor Kim. I will pray about it and let you know." I walked out of the meeting with a skip in my step.

When I got home a few minutes later, I practically threw the door open. This would be a new start.

"Alexandra! I got the job!"

I would be the first Latino member of the Korean church's pastoral staff. In a way it was like becoming a foreign missionary right in my hometown.

44

GOING GLOBAL

A deacon at Promise Church approached me one day. "Pastor Mendoza, we need you internationally. Pastor Kim wants to take the vision of the 4/14 Window Movement worldwide. I know you're already working very hard with PowerHouse Kids, but how would you like to become the leader of PowerHouse Kids International? You could help change the lives of children worldwide."

Surprise must have registered on my face because he added, "I do understand if you would prefer to remain local, given your family."

To be honest, I hadn't actually thought in that moment about how it would affect my family. But now that he'd brought it up, I knew I needed to talk with Alexandra so we could pray about it together.

"Well?" I asked Alexandra after we had talked. "What do you think?"

We had spent some time in prayer and had been listening for God's answer.

"I think God's been preparing you for this. Just like He always does. And I am here to take care of the kids. I can even keep the local program going so you can travel."

It all seemed right. A peace filled my heart. I didn't know quite how this next chapter would look, but I knew that God would be with me wherever I went. And He would be here with Alexandra and the kids, caring for them in my absence.

I couldn't help but remember again Daniel McCarthy's prophecy: "You will be traveling around the world. You will meet public figures that will render their services to you for the advancement of the kingdom of God." It had played out in a myriad of ways and continued to show how all the twists and turns in my life were part of God's plan all along.

A little while later, Pastor Kim shared an idea with me. The plan was to connect with leaders in different countries and introduce them to the concepts and strategies we had developed for children's ministries. We wanted to equip other ministries with the tools to organize and run programs like those we ran through PowerHouse Kids. Our goal was to have a number of leaders pledge to focus on reaching children with the gospel of Christ for at least ten years.

Pastor Kim visited Central and South America to promote the 4/14 Window Movement, and we followed up with training. The first stop was Uruguay, commonly considered the most secular nation in the Americas. So we were surprised when more than one hundred fifty leaders and missionaries signed up for our very first 4/14 Window leadership seminar training.

After the success in Uruguay, we began working out the details to take the training to other countries.

In the Dominican Republic, 173 church leaders registered, an astounding number considering the size of the country. Then we went to Guatemala and held the conference in an area where over 37 dialects were spoken.

Pastor Kim felt God leading him to Venezuela. It seemed as if the timing were incredibly important. He had a sense of urgency to reach the children there before it was too late. He wanted to do things a little differently and set the goal to have 250 leaders attend the seminars.

Working with a connection in the Assemblies of God in Venezuela, we gathered over 270 pastors, teachers, and leaders for our ten-day training event. Pastor Kim discussed the importance of children; his passion to see the next generation grow up in the saving knowledge of Christ was contagious, inspiring even the most tired of ministers.

While in Venezuela, we arranged special games at the soccer stadiums and invited hundreds of children to attend. We packed the house every time! Thousands of children filled the stands to watch their favorite players and hear the message. Millions more watched on television.

It was mind-blowing to look at the stands and watch a sea of people listening to the gospel. I wonder if that was how the disciples felt when thousands came to listen to Jesus.

What a blessing to share the gospel at outreach events worldwide like this soccer game.

Each country presented different challenges. Venezuela had been on the brink of chaos for years, even before the passing of President Hugo Chávez. Colombia's high elevations made us all feel sluggish and headachy. But Chile had such a big demand for the seminar that we went back several times.

45

The Shadow of Death

"I'd like it if you would host a lunch for some of the leaders from Colombia," Pastor Kim said in one of our morning meetings. "Their church sponsored us when we came through Colombia with the *His Life* musical and the soccer crusade. We want them to know how much we appreciate it."

As soon as our meeting was over I called a fantastic Korean restaurant in Flushing and reserved a special dining area. On the day of the lunch, when we were all seated and some of the typical pleasantries were out of the way, I got to talking with a young pastor from Cali, Colombia, who sat across from me.

"You said you're from Cali?" I asked. "Have you ever heard of a guy by the name of Don Sergio?"

He looked at me in surprise. "Yeah. He was super rich. I used to play in his mansion as a kid."

I couldn't believe the connection. Don Sergio had been one of our main drug suppliers. Even though I'd never met him, he had met my brother. I knew his nephew, so it felt like there was a real connection.

"Did you hear he was killed?"

I hadn't. For some reason, the news hit me like a hammer to the chest. In the back of my mind I couldn't help but think, *That could have been me.*

The young pastor looked a little sad as he went on. "I only found out later what he did, how he made all that money. He was always really nice to my friends and me. I was a poor kid in the neighborhood. He used to open up his grounds and let us ride horses, play with his animals. Even bought some pint-sized ATVs and let us ride them all over his property. I really liked him."

I played with my food a little before asking, "When did he . . . how did he . . . die?"

The young pastor shook his head. "Two thousand seven . . . so seven years ago now? It was crazy, really. He was shot over eight times."

I sighed. As far as I knew he had died without giving his life to Christ. Romans 6:23 popped into my head: "For the wages of sin is death, but the free gift of God is eternal life through Christ Jesus our Lord" (TLB). God had spared my life in so many ways. The best thing that ever happened to me was being thrown into the same prison unit with Emilio. It was there in the shadows that God's grace got ahold of me.

Something was wrong with Mami. As usual, she rarely complained about anything, but she was more and more tired lately. She didn't have much of an appetite whenever we had meals together.

On the same day that my grandson Eden was born, my mother was rushed to the hospital with abdominal pain.

"It's cancer."

Those words hit me like a ton of bricks.

"How bad is it?" I asked the doctor.

"There are still a lot of tests to do," he said, "but it doesn't look good."

I was glad I was sitting down. If I wasn't, my knees might have given way. It wasn't that I didn't trust God with my mother's life. I did. But I realized it could be that He felt it was time to take her home, and I just couldn't imagine life without her.

Life can seem so fragile sometimes. Even knowing that God has all our days marked out for us doesn't keep us from feeling like death crouches at the door, ready to overwhelm its next victim as soon as the opportunity arises.

Please, God, no, I begged in silent prayer. *Please give her time.*

46

Mami Goes Home

Mami fought cancer like a champion.

My brothers, Alexandra, and I made sure one of us was always available to take her to chemo treatments.

On my turn, I would sit with her and try my best to smile and chat. I told her all about Samantha, Adam, and Penelope. Mami was as proud of them as Alexandra and I were. Sam had gotten married a few years before and had two sons of her own.

Mami winced a little as the nurse inserted the IV, but then she smiled and talked happily about whatever came to mind. "I'm proud of you, Herman. You know that?"

I tried to chuckle. "Really, Mami? Even after all the grief I gave you as a kid?"

She rubbed my hand. "You aren't that same boy. You serve God now, and I know I don't have to worry about you anymore."

"Do you remember putting me on that plane to D.R. when I was a kid?"

She nodded. "Of course I do. You gave me such headaches back then. I really didn't know what else to do. I felt so bad, tricking you like that. It was hard for me to hand you over to that flight attendant. But I knew you had to be away from the neighborhood. I thought if you spent some time with my papi, he would help set you straight."

"I didn't like it then, but I am grateful for it now."

Mami turned my hand over and rubbed my palm. "God rescued you. . . . You keep living for Him."

The words were precious. The treatment went markedly slow. I knew she was in pain. Her smiles were for my sake; she didn't want her baby to feel sad . . . but I couldn't help it. Even as the minute hand seemed to stay still, I felt like time was going much too quickly.

It didn't help that life was always busy. I was traveling so much with church I wasn't always there to see what she was going through, but I noticed at one point that she started wearing a wig. She was stronger than the doctors had predicted, living beyond their expectations. But she wasn't cured. She grew thinner and weaker. I ached for her as I watched chemo steal her hair and her appetite.

By Christmas of 2018, Mami had grown desperately ill. As I had in the beginning, I still trusted that God could heal her of the cancer. But I also knew that it might just be the means by which He was calling her home. I knew it . . . but I didn't want it.

"Do you remember what the nurse said last time?" Alexandra asked as we drove to Mami's house.

I tried to think back, but we had been given a lot of information in a very short time.

"She said we are in for a long, tough road."

It was an understatement. The previous year, Alexandra's own father succumbed to cancer at the same time that we moved to a house outside the city. We had been traveling so much to different countries with the 4/14 Window Movement that we hadn't had time to think or grieve properly. But through it all, God had faithfully kept us and carried us through the hardest moments, and He would again.

My brothers and I had been taking turns being with Mami around the clock. Alexandra and I were tired. It had been a long week, and work seemed never ending. But moments with Mami were precious; tomorrow was not guaranteed.

When we got to the house, we could see Mami had grown much weaker than she had been just the other day.

"Hola, Mami." I gave her a hug, and she could barely lift her arms to hug me back. "I'll make you something to eat."

Alexandra followed me. "Something's really wrong, Herman. Do you see how yellow she looks?" Alexandra's face reflected the same concern I felt. "I'll check her blood pressure."

I gathered ingredients so I could make Mami her smoothie while the familiar sound of the blood pressure machine came from the other room.

"Herman!"

I didn't like the foreboding tone in Alexandra's voice.

"Seventy over fifty-four. We should take her in."

Mami waved a hand. "I don't want to go in right now. Just give me something with salt. It will bring my blood pressure back up."

We quickly made some soup. She had a spoonful or two and a couple sips of tea, but she looked like she wouldn't keep them down.

Alexandra's voice was firm. "We have to take you to the hospital. It can't wait."

We helped Mami into her sweat pants and jacket. Even in March, the winter winds off the Atlantic chilled this part of New York.

I lifted Mami up to carry her to the car. She felt so small in my arms. Alexandra led the way, opening doors.

On the threshold, Mami said, "Hold on a minute." She looked back at her home, then gave a little nod. Alexandra would say later that it was as if Mami were saying good-bye.

Alexandra helped her into the back seat and, sitting beside her, buckled her in. As soon as they were both settled I pressed the gas pedal, and we took off down the narrow streets. I turned on the hazard lights and tried to wind my way between the tightly packed vehicles lining our route.

I was ready to breathe a sigh of relief, when we noticed flashing lights. The road was blocked and state troopers were redirecting traffic. We didn't have time for a detour. I pulled up to the blockade and rolled down my window.

"What's going on? Is there no way we can get through?"

The trooper shook his head. "We've got an electrical pole down and blocking the road. We can't let anything past."

I fished in the glove compartment and grabbed my chaplain badge. "Can't you make a way? I have an emergency."

He looked at the badge and then back at me. I'm sure my worry for Mami was written plainly in my eyes as they begged him to have mercy on us.

He gave a nod and waved me through.

We made it past the power pole to the ER. In less than a minute I was wheeling Mami in.

It was several weeks before her condition stabilized. Then, just as we were waiting to get the discharge notice, she began to vomit. It was an ominous shade of black. We pressed the call button, and nurses quickly arrived to help. There were a hushed scramble and whispers of old blood and kidney fluid. I didn't know exactly what that meant, but it obviously wasn't good.

The doctor came in shortly after, his face grave. "I'm afraid we can't send her home."

My brothers arrived, and the doctor said to all of us, "Medically speaking, there's nothing we can do. The tumor has taken over 90 percent of her liver. She isn't getting enough nutrients, but we can't remove it at this stage. It would be wise to get ready to say your good-byes."

"How much time does she have?" one of my brothers asked.

Even knowing it was a question only God could answer, I wanted the doctor to say we had more time than I feared.

"Days . . . maybe weeks," the doctor said. "It is hard to tell at this point."

Leaving the meeting, we knew we needed to start funeral arrangements. We wanted to know our mother's wishes and abide by them. Someone would have to talk with Mami.

"I can do it," Fabian offered.

I was glad it wouldn't have to be me.

Mami took the news so much better than I expected. In fact, she did her best to be optimistic and bright so that we wouldn't be sad.

"We're trusting in God, Mami . . . but we want to do everything we can to make your days comfortable," Emilio told her, squeezing her hand.

"Gracias, mis hijos," she thanked us, her big brown eyes brimming with affection.

A lump rose in my throat. I tried to swallow it, but it wouldn't budge. As much as I could, I would be with Mami in these last moments.

During one of Papi's visits to Mami's hospital room, his feebleness was noticeable to my siblings and me. He looked depleted. As he made his way to her bedside, we made room for him to take a moment to reflect and whisper in her ear. It was something he had become accustomed to doing during his prayer time while visiting Mami. As I observed his movements and how he touched her hand, it was obvious to me that he was praying over her.

I had never imagined that Mami, a woman of such strength, would look so delicate. I thought about how many years of marriage they had been blessed with and how devastated Papi would be by her loss.

Alexandra gave Mami a foot rub, and I recorded a conversation with her, asking her questions about her family and the early years of her life.

She couldn't help but add, "I love my daughter-in-law. Someday, I will be waiting for her at the gates of heaven. But not too soon. Her husband, children, and grandchildren rely on her. They need her too much. But someday, I will welcome her with open arms."

I asked, "What about me, Mami?"

She chuckled. "Oh, you know I will. And with arms wide open I will say, '¡Hola, mi Herman!'"

A little while later, Mami said, "I want you to call someone for me."

It had become a familiar request in the last few days. She was systematically calling every family member to say her last good-byes.

She gave me the next name on her list, and I passed along her request for them to visit her in the hospital. With each one, it was the same—they came to her bedside and she looked them in the eyes and said, "Please forgive me for anything I have done toward you. I love you." They also asked Mami for her forgiveness for any offenses that they might have committed against her.

In those moments, I saw the love of Jesus working through her. The forgiveness and love she offered could only be possible through Him. They were beautiful, soul-cleansing good-byes.

Mami modeled loyalty, and her smile and laughter lightened the atmosphere. Her smile had the ability to improve your day . . . and for some, it helped them through very difficult times.

It was an honor and a privilege to sit with Mami for those good-byes. Even in the moments that were hard to watch or be a part of, I felt blessed that I could be with her.

"He leads me beside quiet waters, he refreshes my soul." I whispered Psalm 23 into Mami's ear. It had been a while since she had spoken, but sometimes when I recited or read the Bible to her, tears would trickle down her face.

Please, God, I prayed, *can I just hear her speak once more before you take her?* The thought that I might never hear her voice again was too much to bear.

It was four in the morning when God answered my prayer. Dante (who had been released back in 2000), Alexandra, and I were all there, keeping watch through the night.

Suddenly, Mami extended her hands in the air and said, "Lord!"

My heart fluttered in my chest, and I ran to her side. I took her hand in mine.

"I'm tired," she said. "Please take me home, but let it be your will, not mine."

"Mami, I'm here." *Please look at me,* my heart begged.

She turned her head slightly to look at Dante and me. "You, my sons, are my pearls . . . love one another. Walk with integrity. Honor God and hold on to your family name with integrity. Show honesty, respect, and love for others."

Her hands dropped back to her sides, and she fell back to sleep. It was the last time we heard her voice.

I had prayed that I wouldn't be in the room when Mami went home to heaven. There were others who wanted to be there—she didn't have to be alone . . . but I really didn't think my heart could take it.

We all knew she was ready to go, but how were we to reconcile ourselves to the fact that we wouldn't see our mother again—that we would only hear her voice in recordings, only see her smile in pictures?

Please, God . . . I can't handle seeing her go.

But God answered no.

It was March 17, 2018. Alexandra and I were taking our turn at her side.

I whispered in Mami's ear, "I'm here. I love you, Mami. . . . God loves you. God loves you."

She let out a soft groan, and I felt myself begin to tear up. I turned to Alexandra. "I don't think I can handle this."

She rubbed my arms. "Why don't you step out for a minute. I'll be here."

I escaped into the hallway and called my brothers. We'd been spending a lot of time together the last few weeks. We would debrief on the day's events and share how we felt Mami was doing. Just talking it out really helped. We were stronger when we were strong for each other.

When I came back to the room, I felt a little calmer. The panicked desire to break into tears had dissipated. A chaplain stopped by, and we chatted about Mami's condition. Before he left, we asked if he would pray with us, which he did willingly.

He had just walked out when my son, Adam, came in. I had told him he didn't need to come. He'd had a busy day tutoring, but he insisted on coming.

Adam joined Alexandra at Mami's bedside, told Mami he loved her, and asked for her blessing.

Alexandra had been staring at Mami when all of a sudden I heard her say, "Herman! It's time."

Mami had suddenly opened her eyes.

I hoped she was wrong. I felt frozen.

"Come, Herman. Read her Psalm 23."

I couldn't think for myself in that moment. I didn't want to think about anything, really. I grabbed my Bible and began to read. I had barely gotten through the first verses when her eyes closed and her jaw slackened.

She was gone.

We knew it even before the doctor came in and checked her vitals. No pulse. No breath. He turned to us with real compassion in his eyes. "I'm sorry for your loss." He recorded her time of death as 6:30 P.M.

I was surprised at the feeling of peace that came over me in those moments. I had cried like a baby the last few days and thought I really wouldn't be able to handle being there. But God revealed to me just how capable He is at carrying us through life's hardest moments. I called my brothers, feeling quite calm.

They arrived quickly, and we gathered around Mami. The medical staff finished some paper work and allowed us a few hours with her.

We crowded around the bed. We prayed for each other and then sang a favorite song. When the last note faded, we fell into a hushed silence.

47

THE PRESENT

My family means everything to me. Less than a year after my mother's funeral, I lost my dad to a massive heart attack. I thank God for the opportunity He gave me to spend the last few days with my dad before he passed.

When I was still in prison, I prayed for my family's salvation, knowing the Word of God could reach them even when I could not, and they are all now serving God. Dante owns dozens of laundromats across the New York City area. Emilio is an entrepreneur and owns a construction company. They are both doing very well.

My wife, Alexandra, holds me up as only a godly woman can. She works alongside me for God's kingdom.

Samantha, my eldest, started her own business and also works with me at our church. She ministers and teaches arts and crafts at PowerHouse Kids. She is the proud mom of two boys. One of my happiest moments is seeing my grandchildren, Chase and Eden, reciting Bible verses and worshiping the Lord. God's salvation and grace is being passed down to the next generation of my family.

My son, Adam, is currently working for the Federal Aviation Administration and enjoys playing basketball, tutoring, and teaching at PowerHouse Kids.

My youngest, Penelope, always brightens my day with her beautiful smile. She is a dental assistant and loves fashion and photography.

My family (from left to right): Adam, Samantha, Eden, Chase, Alexandra, and Penelope.

About a year ago, I invited a good friend, Dr. Joel Freeman, to deliver a sermon at Promise Ministries. I'll never forget the illustration he used to make the point that we can never truly put ourselves in another person's place.

Joel pulled out a massive shoe belonging to Shaquille O'Neal. It was a size 22 and measured a staggering sixteen inches. Shaq's shoes and his experiences wouldn't fit anyone else. I could never wear Shaq's sneakers. No matter what I might try, they wouldn't fit. But Shaq can't wear mine either. I understood two points. First, it is important to remember that we have no idea what has happened in someone's life to bring them to where they are now. And second, every person must take full responsibility for their own actions and decisions.

I am thankful to God for the shoes I walk in today. I am the director of PowerHouse Kids, a program of Promise Ministries International that provides kids in the community with music, art, academic, and sports classes to help them stay off the streets and encourage them to engage their God-given talents to become successful adults. As a speaker for the 4/14 Window Global Movement, I frequently address leaders about the importance of reaching children and youth for Jesus.

I am constantly amazed by the life and adventure God has led me into. He is good. All the time. And everything good in me is from Him. Thanks be to God, I have shared the good news in over thirty countries.

I encourage you to consider what kind of influence you have on others, what direction your shoes are taking you, and whether you are walking on the path that leads to joy and purpose. No matter what situation you may be in today, God can lead you to victory.

My story is a testament that God can rescue you from whatever condition you may be in, regardless of how the shadows have shifted in your past. Even now He invites you to enter the fullness of His kingdom through repentance and receiving His forgiveness. The Lord Jesus longs to see you come to a place of spiritual freedom; His truth does not shift, but instead lights the way to a life of joy and purpose. Say yes to Jesus, and you will experience a life transformed!

ACKNOWLEDGMENTS

There are so many people whom the Lord has used to mentor me, guide me, and shape me into the man I am today. They offered support throughout my life, and for that I am thankful.

To my Lord and Savior Jesus Christ, who gave His life in order that I may live, thank you. Without you I am nothing, and as my wife once said, I don't know how to live without you. Words cannot express how grateful I am, to you, my Father, for saving me.

My Family

My wife, Alexandra, an extraordinary woman of God, exemplifies faithfulness and love. She is truly a woman after God's own heart. Love you, baby.

My children—Samantha, Adam, and Penelope—you are such a blessing in my life, and watching you grow and become productive and successful adults is a testament to the Scripture that says, "Believe on the Lord Jesus Christ, and you will be saved, you and your household" (Acts 16:31 NKJV).

My grandsons, Chase and Eden, your fervent desire to worship God at such a young age is so special for me to watch. I look forward to seeing how God will use you for His kingdom as you grow up.

To my mom, who offered so much support in the beginning stages of this project, you were truly a Proverbs 31 woman, and how you kept your faith in Jesus during your most difficult trials will always be engraved on my heart. I love you, Mami. Till we meet again. Also my dad, who fervently prayed for me everywhere I went. Your love for God's Word will always be an inspiration to me. And to my aunt Rosa Francia Ortiz, who was like my second mom. I know that one day I will see you all again in heaven.

To my four brothers and their families, whom I love dearly, and my wife's family, who supported her and my kids while I was away, thank you.

My Friends

Cliff Jean-Philippe, Gloria Messam, and Robert Garcia, who have worked with me for so many years in ministry, you guys were always willing to go wherever God sent us. My buddy Will Flores, your prayers for me during the writing of this book meant so much. Randy Brooks and Grace Schienbein, thank you for spending countless hours with me editing and revising the manuscript. Thanks to Pastor Joshua Mayen and Reverend Kimberly Wright for being such supportive friends. Eva and Gabriel Guardarramas, I'm so grateful to you for opening your house to me and supporting the ministry.

My Spiritual Mentors

Reverend Leroy Ricksy, my spiritual dad, who took the time to minister to me while I was in prison when I was just a baby in Christ, you followed through even after my release and taught me how important it is to walk with integrity. Reverend Nam Soo Kim, my second spiritual dad, who showed me a new level of walking by faith, you never held my past against me but instead offered me an opportunity to work in God's house and allowed me to soar. A heartfelt thank-you to Bishop Dorcilien and Maman Bishop, who were instrumental in helping me provide humanitarian aid to Haiti; Reverend Gilberto Pichardo, whom God uses whenever I need sound advice; and Reverend Dennis Bloom and his wife, who took my family in and served as spiritual mentors to my wife and children.

Prison Ministries and Mentors

I want to acknowledge the support from Robert De la Torre, who took the time to visit and preach to me while I was in prison; Chaplain Peter Levasseur, who helped us organize our church in prison; my spiritual momma, Mrs. Betty General; Captain Alfonso Bonilla; and Reverend Jose Torres. I also want to thank Gideons International, Prison Fellowship, and Pastor Lloyd Pulley for sending Bibles to 5-North.

Promise Ministries International

Thank you to Senior Pastor Reverend Ben Hur, my coworkers at Promise Ministries International, and the members of Promise Church.

And to the countless others, who in one way or another contributed to my spiritual growth, thank you.

About the Author

Herman A. Mendoza was born in Queens, New York, to Dominican immigrants. The youngest of five boys living in a rough neighborhood, Herman was caught up in the gang and drug culture and served time for running a drug business. In prison, Herman gave his life to Christ, studied theology, and copastored a growing in-prison church.

In the early 2000s, he was acknowledged for his humanitarian efforts in Port-au-Prince, Haiti, and the Dominican Republic. These efforts became known as the One Voice movement and led to speaking engagements at Fortune 500 companies as well as Columbia University.

At public schools, Herman engages with young people on the dangers of drugs and gangs. He has spoken on several televised programs, including CBN's *The 700 Club* and TBN's *Praise the Lord*. He also spearheaded a United Nations event with special guest Allan Houston.

Herman currently serves as an associate pastor at Promise Ministries International and leads the growth and development of the 4/14 Window best practices program, PowerHouse Kids, under the direction of Pastor Nam Soo Kim. The 4/14 Window Global Movement seeks to raise a new generation of children, ages four to fourteen, to be the leaders of tomorrow through Jesus Christ.

Herman lives in Long Island, New York, with his wife, Alexandra. They have three grown children and two grandsons.